Gods, Goddesses, and Mythology

Volume 8

Oceania–Poseidon

Marshall Cavendish
New York • London • Singapore

Marshall Cavendish
99 White Plains Road
Tarrytown, New York 10591

www.marshallcavendish.us

Library of Congress Cataloging-in-Publication Data

Gods, goddesses, and mythology/editor, C. Scott Littleton.
    p. cm.
    Includes bibliographical references and index.
    ISBN 0-7614-7559-1 (set : alk. paper)
1. Mythology--Encyclopedias. I. Littleton, C. Scott. II. Marshall
Cavendish Corporation. III. Title.

    BL312.G64 2005
    201'.3'03--dc22

2004040758

ISBN 0-7614-7559-1 (set)
ISBN 0-7614-7567-2 (vol. 8)

Printed and bound in China

09 08 07 06 05   6 5 4 3 2

General Editor
C. Scott Littleton, Occidental College, Los Angeles

Marshall Cavendish
Project Editor: Marian Armstrong
Editorial Director: Paul Bernabeo
Production Manager: Alan Tsai

Brown Reference Group
Project Editor: Chris King
Editors: Henry Russell, Dawn Titmus, Tom Webber
Designer: Steve Wilson
Picture Researcher: Helen Simm
Cartographer: Mark Walker
Indexer: Kay Ollerenshaw
Managing Editor: Tim Cooke

Picture Credits

CONTENTS

OCEANIA

Spread across one third of Earth's surface, the 25,000 islands of Oceania are so remote that their inhabitants had little contact with each other— and none with the developed world— until the 16th century CE. Despite their isolation, however, the social and religious systems that developed across the Pacific Ocean have some fascinating common threads.

Below: This small island is one of many in a group called the Cook Islands. Oceania is made up of many different groups of islands.

Oceania is the collective name given to the islands of the Pacific Ocean, including New Zealand and sometimes Australia. The people who live on the many scattered islands group themselves into three geographical and cultural areas: Polynesia, Melanesia, and Micronesia. Polynesians inhabit the triangle of islands from New Zealand north to Hawaii and east to Easter Island; Melanesian people predominate on the island of New Guinea, nearby archipelagos, and the Fiji Islands. Micronesia is made up of the scattering of islands north of the equator.

The first humans settled in the islands of the Pacific at least 40,000 years ago. Waves of settlers arrived at later dates from what is now Southeast Asia and also from Australia. Their lifestyles varied depending on the type of island on which they lived: some islands were large and supported extensive rain forests that could be cleared for agriculture. Others were mountainous and had little arable land. For many of the islanders, particularly around the coasts, the

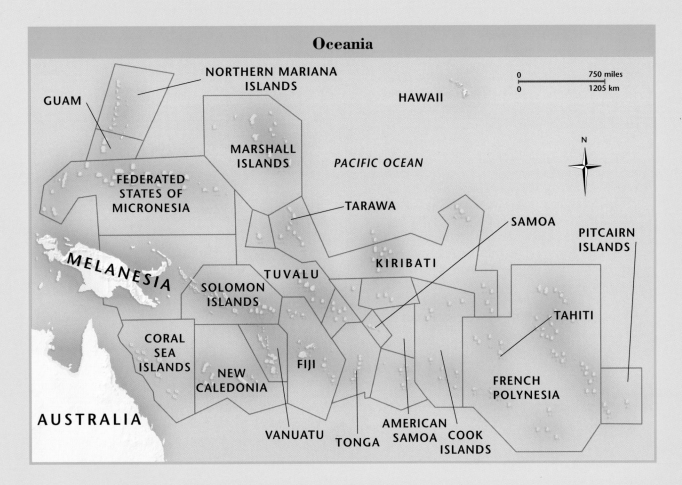

Oceania

NORTHERN MARIANA
ISLANDS

GUAM

HAWAII

0   750 miles
0   1205 km

PACIFIC OCEAN

N

MARSHALL
ISLANDS

FEDERATED
STATES OF
MICRONESIA

TARAWA

SAMOA

PITCAIRN
ISLANDS

MELANESIA

KIRIBATI

TUVALU

SOLOMON
ISLANDS

TAHITI

CORAL
SEA
ISLANDS

FIJI

NEW
CALEDONIA

FRENCH
POLYNESIA

AUSTRALIA

VANUATU   TONGA

AMERICAN
SAMOA   COOK
ISLANDS

dominant influence on their lives was the Pacific Ocean. It was a source of fish and seafood. It both isolated islands from their neighbors and provided a highway for travel in outrigger canoes or on rafts; the inhabitants of the islands were skilled navigators. The ocean's waters could lap gently at the shore but could also be whipped up into furious storms called typhoons.

Despite centuries of habitation, Oceania had little recorded history before the arrival of Europeans in the early 16th century. Contact with Christianity and in some cases the tradition of fierce warfare between communities have eroded traditional indigenous belief systems. Today, however, native religion and customs are being resurrected, especially in Australia, New Zealand, and Hawaii.

Polynesian religion

Throughout Polynesia two concepts were the bedrock of religion and have passed into Western culture. One was mana, the sacred power that surrounds royalty, ancestors, and heroes. The other was the concept of *tapu* (taboo)— that is, the idea that certain relationships and sacred objects are protected by a prohibition against touch or misuse. People who broke the rules could only be taken back into the community by sacrificial acts.

Honor and kinship were primary values, as was the ancestral power that went back to the gods themselves. The creation myth of the Maori people of New Zealand told of an unbroken continuum that connected the original divine thought to the making of the earth, the begetting of life, and finally to the great ancestors.

The Polynesian peoples believed that the two great forces of the universe were Ao and Po. For Hawaiians, Maoris, and Tahitians, Ao was the male principle of the sky while Po was the female principle of the earth. As in Greek and western Asian mythology, the heavens were associated with day and masculinity, while the earth was linked with night and femininity. Somewhere in between was the terrifying volcano goddess, Pele, now more commonly known as Madame Pele. Po was not associated with evil, terror, and darkness, but was a warm, nourishing mother. She was also associated with dreams, lovemaking, and spirits, making her power a source of intuition.

In the beginning, the Hawaiians say, was a chaotic ocean. The sky god Ku chanted creation into being. First he separated the two great forces, Ao and Po, so that day and night were distinct from each other. Ku created the squid, and this animal later became god of the sea and was called Kanaloa. Kanaloa's son was the trickster Maui.

Importance of Birdsong

The music of Oceania echoes the people's attachment to the natural world. The sounds of flutes and panpipes—reminiscent of birdsong—are reminders that nature is the source of all life.

In Rarotonga, in the Cook Islands, the story of the lovers Pararo and Inutoto describes the unity of nature and love. While Pararo went fishing in his canoe, Inutoto attended a dance to which her husband had forbidden her to go. Pararo, unable to catch anything, went to the dance and dragged his wife away. She was so furious and embarrassed that she decided to leave him. Pararo awoke and found his wife gone. Led by a bird, he tracked Inutoto into a forest cave where she was hiding. He found her there and the two were reconciled. Ever after, the song of the reconciling bird was sacred to lovers wishing to find each other again.

Above: These open tube flutes are called nguru *by Maori people. A melodious sound is produced when air is blown across the upper hole; they are often played to accompany a spoken poem or tale.*

The sky god Ku and the earth and underworld goddess, Hina, were the parents of all the other gods in the Polynesian pantheon. The name Ku means "rising upright" and has a double meaning: it refers both to the rising sun and the phallus. The name Hina means "leaning down" and refers to the setting sun, although Hina was also associated with the moon. When worshipers prayed to Ku, they turned east; when they prayed to Hina, they faced west.

Ku also created the first man, called Kane in Hawaii and Tane in New Zealand. In some versions Kane is the son of Ku and Hina, a relationship that makes him a semidivine figure. Kane fathered reptiles, rivers, and plants with other beings, but most of all he wanted to father a child. He took soft, red clay from Hawaiki, the Polynesians' mythic homeland, and from it created a woman, Hine Hauk Ona, meaning "woman formed of earth."

The couple produced a daughter, Hine Titama, which means "dawn woman." She was so beautiful that her father made her his secret wife, which was a taboo relationship. He did not tell her that he was her father, but eventually she learned the truth.

Hine Hauk Ona was horrified when her daughter told her the story of Kane's incest. "You have broken the umbilical cord of the world," Hine Hauk Ona lamented to Kane, "and must never touch your daughter again." To ensure that her command would be obeyed, Hine Hauk Ona took her daughter to be a co-queen of the underworld, and there the two women stayed, well out of Kane's reach.

Kane himself was never allowed under the earth, and his children, all humanity, had to live out their lives in the harsh realm of Ao, split from the warmth and love of Po. Only when they died could they rejoin the motherly principle and dwell in the underworld.

Maori creation myths

In New Zealand the Maori people believed that Rangi, the sky god, and the earth mother, Papatuanuku, were the creators. The two produced 70 children, all of them gods. Because the Ao and Po forces were not yet divided, the 70 children were packed tightly together like sardines. One of them, Tu Matauenga, suggested they kill their father to make more room. Tu Matauenga was a god of conflict, much like the Greek deity Ares. Another suggestion was offered by Tane Mahuta, the forest god, who said, "Why don't we just lift Father Rangi up gently, so that he will be high above Papatuanuku, our mother? Then there will be plenty of room for all of us."

The gods decided that Tane Mahuta's idea was best, but with all their combined effort they could lift the sky only as high as a taro plant. The sea god Tangaroa (known as the squid god Kanaloa in Hawaii) pushed as hard as he could with a great sea wave, but the sky was still too low. The god of wild-food plants, Huma Tikitiki, could only manage to lift the sky to the height of a banana plant.

The gods were stumped and sat around wondering what to do. The wise forest god, Tane Mahuta, decided to try once more. He lay on the earth and pushed the sky upward with legs that were strong as tree trunks. While he was pushing, he could hear the screams of his parents as they were forced apart. According to the myth, Father Rangi's tears still flow as morning dew whenever he thinks about his separation from his wife. As a result of Tane Mahuta's efforts, however, there was plenty of room on earth for all forms of life. The Chatham Islanders shared the same basic story but added a third being, Ranitokona, which means "the being who holds up the sky." Ranitokona made 10 pillars that held the sky, and he also made the first man.

The trickster Maui also took a turn at keeping the sky up. One day he spied a beautiful young girl who was trying to push the sky higher. She complained that it kept falling on her as she tried to do her chores. Maui bragged

Below: These stone figures stand on Easter Island in eastern Polynesia. Islanders believe they represent ancestral chiefs whose continuing presence protects the community.

Deities and Heroes

Haumea:	Hawaiian fertility goddess.
Hina/Hine:	Polynesian earth, underworld, and moon goddess.
Ku:	Hawaiian creator god.
Maui:	Polynesian hero and trickster.
Ngendi:	Fijian serpentine creator god.
Olofat:	Micronesian hero.
Oro:	Tahitian war god.
Papatuanuku:	Polynesian earth and underworld goddess, mother of the gods.
Pele:	Polynesian fire and volcano goddess.
Qat:	Melanesian hero.
Rangi:	Maori father/sky god.
Tane Mahuta:	Maori forest god.
Tangaroa/Kanaloa:	Polynesian sea god.
To Kabinana:	Melanesian creator hero.
Tu Matauenga:	Maori god of conflict.

that he could lift the sky, but the girl mocked him. Maui said, "I am the son of the god Tangaroa. Though my mother is only a mortal, I have divine power. If you make love with me, I will push the sky up for you." Since Maui was charming, the girl agreed. Maui's success at this task made him conceited, however, and in the end it brought him trouble.

Although his mother had warned Maui not to annoy his great-great-grandmother, Mahui-Ike, he insisted on going to the underworld to visit her. She was the keeper of the fire. Maui went deep into a cave and wandered until he came to Mahui-Ike's home. There he charmed her with sweet words and his handsome face until she agreed to give him a fingernail of flame. He took her fingernail but doused it in water when he came above ground. Then he went down again and explained that the flame had gone out. His ancestor gladly gave him another of her fingernails, but the trickster kept on dousing the flame and coming back for another nail.

In the end Mahui-Ike had only one nail left. She flung it at her naughty great-great-grandson and told him he would get more fire than he bargained for. A great fire sprang up on earth, and Maui transformed into an eagle in order to escape it. At last he begged his father, Tangaroa, to rain on the fire and put it out, and the earth was saved.

Maui's quest for immortality

In a New Zealand Maori story, Maui was condemned to death when he cruelly turned his brother-in-law into a dog. Since Maui was the son of a god, his father Tangaroa advised him to seek out Hina, keeper of the underworld, and obtain mercy.

Maui, for his part, resented the power of Hina to decide who lived and who died. He crawled between the sleeping goddess's legs and rose up inside her body, coming out of her mouth. He knew that if he could do this daring deed twice, he would become immortal. He tried it again, but this time a bird laughed so loudly at the sight that the goddess woke up. She was furious with Maui for his arrogance and crushed him to death. After Maui's foolish mistake, no human has achieved immortality.

Despite his misadventures, Maui was also known for great deeds, such as pulling up whole islands as he fished, bringing fire to the earth (like the Greek Prometheus), and making the sun slow in its course across the sky.

Oceanian deities

The gods of Oceania took various forms but carried out similar functions. Each divinity represented a single aspect of nature, although some ruled over larger domains than others. A number of them had great influence over the fate of humans, both for good or ill. The minor deities were attached to particular volcanoes, islands, streams, or mountains. A spirit dwelled in every stone or spring.

Because the islands are widely separated by ocean, however, over the centuries wide regional variations

Tangaroa and Io

Tangaroa was known throughout Polynesia as the sea god. In Samoa and Tonga (as Tangaloa) and in Tahiti (as Ta'aroa), he was worshiped as a supreme being, father of gods and human beings. According to the Tahitians, he created the universe after breaking out of a shell that existed in a void. He formed the sky from part of the shell and made earth from the rest. He used his own body to make living things.

The best-known creator figure in New Zealand was Io, whose stories parallel the Christian account of creation. Io made light out of watery darkness by speaking sacred words. No images of the god have survived, if any were made, and he was rarely mentioned in prayers and chants.

Above: This 18th- or 19th-century wooden figure is from Rarotonga, one of the Cook Islands. It has been suggested that this is a statue of the god of creation, Tangaroa.

Below: This lintel from a doorway in New Zealand is carved from wood. Maori identify the central figure as Papatuanuku, the earth mother.

emerged in the forms the gods and stories took. Tangaroa, for example, appeared in Micronesia as Tabu Eriki ("sacred chief"). In the eastern Marshall Islands he was a nameless thunder god. Tangaroa had the qualities of both sexes and could even appear as a sea snake or turtle. In the Cook Islands the creator god Rongo and his three sons may have represented these aspects of Tangaroa—they all brought forth gods and humans. In the Fiji Islands Tangaroa appeared as Ngendi, who caused earthquakes, fertility and sterility, and fire. Ngendi was also creator of the gods, earth, and, according to some island groups, humans. Ngendi hatched a huge egg like the world egg of Tangaroa (see box, opposite), according to one version. A Samoan version says that Tuli, the daughter of Tangaroa, was responsible for creation.

The Polynesian agricultural god Lono appeared in various islands as Rongala and Mo Rogrog (meaning "bringing fire from heaven"). Tu, the god of war, was present throughout Polynesia.

Each craft had a god of its own, and the gods of roofs and canoes—items that were particularly important on tropical islands—had especially high status. Tane, son of Rangi the sky god, was a nature god of the forests, and woodworkers would invoke him. Hine was the Polynesian goddess of darkness and the underworld. As Hina, the moon, she was the goddess of women's crafts, such as weaving. The Hawaiian goddess Kapo was the deity of both fertility and abortion, as well as of tattooing and other arts.

Spiritual aspects of nature

The Oceanian arts and myths reflect a need for people to ask forgiveness for what they must do to survive—that is, hunt and kill animals. The Pacific Islanders honored fish and other animals in their stories and dances. A similar relationship between art and hunting existed for the inhabitants of Spain and southern France 18,000 years ago, as evidenced by the cave paintings of sacred hunting scenes at Lascaux in France and Altamira in Spain.

Continuity with the ancestors was the dominant influence on belief systems in Oceania. Boys learned from warrior spirits how to be men. A successful warrior was said to be empowered by the mana of his ancestors, so he would have an important life, full of achievements and honor.

Christian missionaries arrived in the late 18th and early 19th centuries and taught the island peoples to reject their heritage in favor of Christianity. These teachings upset the balance of the islanders' social order—the mana of their ancestors no longer made them strong—and the people often fell victim to disease, alcoholism, and apathy.

In recent years the Christian Church has encouraged islanders to value again traditions such as belief in the spirits of the dead, the twilight of the gods, and the art of tattooing. The church is beginning to understand the importance of the islanders' beliefs in an invisible world and the spiritual aspects of nature.

The story of Tinaicaboga

Naturally the ocean has a huge importance for island people, so it is not surprising that the myths of Oceania are deeply bound to the sea. The story of Tinaicaboga concerns a shape-shifting ancestor spirit who lived in the most ancient times. Tinaicaboga thought about becoming a bird but wanted to be under the waves, not flying over them. So she decided to transform herself into a giant sea turtle and forever flew under the water like a bird.

The early people of Fiji honored Tinaicaboga and rejoiced that the great ancestor had honored them with her presence in the ocean. At a later time, however, men decided to catch the sea turtle and eat her. They caught her in a bag and threw her into the bottom of their canoe.

Below: These two jade fishhook pendants were once worn by important Maori chiefs. They symbolized the fishhook used by Maui, the trickster, to catch the North Island of New Zealand.

Tinaicaboga had magical powers, however, and caused the rising of a great storm, much like the one the Greek sea god Poseidon created. The canoe capsized, drowning the men, and Tinaicaboga escaped into the sea depths. She swam to the island of Kadavu in Fiji and made her home in a lagoon near the village of Namuana. There people respected her presence and were grateful for the songs she taught them.

In another version of the story, Tinaicaboga was a princess who lived in Namuana and liked to go fishing with her daughter, Raudalice. Some men of the village of Nabukelevu caught them in a net and would not let them go, despite their pleas. The gods of the sea helped the women by causing a storm, during which the men were astonished to see the women become giant turtles. When the men threw the turtles into the sea, the storm subsided and the men were saved. The sea turtles turned back into women and swam safely to shore. The message is clear: honor the sea life of the ocean and you will live in peace. The women of Namuana still honor the sacred sea turtle as their ancestor. They climb to the top of the cliffs and sing a song to Tinaicaboga. When she answers their call, the villagers know that no enemies will dare harm them.

Spirits of the dead also had an enduring presence on the islands. The moon spirit Taakura of Rarotonga, in the Cook

Above: A Hawaiian surfer masters a wave in the Pacific Ocean. In Oceanian mythology the first surfboard was carved by Hina, moon goddess of the waves.

Islands, sat on the black rocks, combed her long hair, and dreamed her own dreams. Fishermen sailed by and tried to get her attention, but she ignored them. She was so beautiful that the men felt shy about sharing their catch with her as they shared it with other villagers.

One day a fisherman dared to sneak up and touch Taakura's beautiful long hair as she sat in contemplation. She was angry and pushed him away. In revenge, the local fishermen set her hut on fire and burned her alive. She cursed them and became a ghost that haunted the island, leading men to their deaths by calling them out to sea and drowning them. In this story the danger of the waters and the spirits within them is a reminder to the islanders to respect the powerful sea.

Tales of the ocean

Oceanians were renowned for their skills in the water, and these skills, such as surfing in Tahiti, have entered into modern mythology. In the beginning, according to the Tahitians, Ta'aroa, the creator god, produced many other gods, including Hina, the moon goddess of the waves. She decided to live on earth and walked the forests in search of a tree to make the first surfboard. The uru tree was her choice, and she polished to perfection a surfboard made from it. The king was the first man to use the board, but since then many young Tahitians have perfected the art.

In a parallel to the biblical flood story, the Hawaiians believe that, long ago during a great flood, only the peak of Mauna Kea stood above the waters. On this tiny piece of land stood the only living humans. The story goes that, in the time of the Overturning, there was a great seer called Nana Nu'u. The flood was called the "sea that made the chiefs fall," and Nana Nu'u took this name for himself. He was thereafter called Ku-kapuna, and with his wife, Ku-kekoa, he repopulated the earth. In another version of the story he built an immense boat for his family so that they would survive the flood, but the source of this tale was probably the Christian missionaries' story of Noah's ark.

BARBARA GARDNER

Bibliography

Alpers, Anthony. *Legends of the South Sea*. Christchurch, New Zealand: Whitcombe and Tombs, 1970.

Boutilier, James A., Daniel T. Hughes, and Sharon W. Tiffany. *Mission, Church and Sect in Oceania*. Ann Arbor, MI: University of Michigan Press, 1992.

Campbell, I. C. *Island Kingdom: Tonga Ancient and Modern*. Christchurch, New Zealand: Canterbury University Press, 1992.

SEE ALSO: Ancestor Worship; Australia; Earth Mother; Flood Myths; Moon; Poseidon; Prometheus; Sea.

OCEANUS

In Greek mythology Oceanus was one of the earliest beings to exist in the cosmos. Despite his name, Oceanus was not a personification of the world's oceans. Instead he symbolized the great river that the ancient Greeks believed encircled the earth. He was also the father of an enormous brood of children, 6,000 in all, who comprised some of the basic natural features of the earth's landscape.

Oceanus was the first of the children born to Gaia and Uranus, the personifications of the earth and the sky respectively. Oceanus was thus the eldest of the 12 Titans. However, although he appeared at an early stage of the story of the creation, Oceanus was not the first figure to be associated with water. The ancient Greek account of the creation of the universe, as told by the poet Hesiod (fl. 800 BCE) in his *Theogony*, differentiated between two elemental beings associated with the oceans: Pontus and Oceanus. Of these, Pontus was the elder.

The story of creation

According to the Greek story of the creation of the universe, the first thing to come into being was Chaos, a vast, yawning void. It was followed by Gaia (the earth), Tartarus (a region that lay thousands of miles below the earth's surface), and Eros (sexual attraction). Gaia's first act was to create three fundamental realms in addition to herself. They were Uranus (the sky), Ourea (the mountains) and Pontus (the ocean). The creation of Pontus and his siblings neatly divided the world into four basic realms—earth, sea, sky, and mountains—a division that reflected the geographical nature of Greece itself.

Gaia mated with each of her three offspring in turn. Pontus's coupling with Gaia produced a number of creatures who dwelled in the depths of the ocean. One of the most famous was the sea god Nereus, often known as the Old Man of the Sea, who fathered thousands of sea nymphs, the Nereids.

Oceanus, on the other hand, was one of the next generation of beings to come into existence after the creation of Uranus, Ourea, and Pontus. He was the first of the 12 Titans whom Gaia created by mating with Uranus. Oceanus was not a clumsy duplicate of Pontus. Nor was he a simple embodiment of freshwater, as opposed to the salt water of Pontus. Instead Oceanus represented water as a source of life and vitality. This aspect of the god is reflected in the nature of his many offspring. Unlike the children of Pontus, Oceanus's offspring were not just creatures of the deep. They were beings of great vitality and beauty. Oceanus had 3,000 daughters and 3,000 sons (see box, page 1022). The daughters, known as Oceanids, were nymphs who dwelled in springs and wells, while his sons were rivers that ran through land, providing drinking water and acting as sources of irrigation.

In Greek myth Oceanus is seen less as an embodiment of the sea and more as a world river, encircling the earth. In the *Iliad*, the account of the last year of the Trojan War by Greek poet Homer (c. ninth–eighth century BCE), Hephaestus, blacksmith of the gods, forges new armor for the great Greek warrior Achilles. He decorates Achilles' shield with a representation of the whole world, including the sun, moon, and heavens. Around the rim, encircling all, is the river of Oceanus.

Although Oceanus was one of the Titans, he did not take their side in the battle they fought with the Olympian gods for the control of the universe. Even after the Olympians proved victorious, Oceanus retained his role as the great world river. The Olympian Poseidon took over the sea as his realm, and to some extent replaced Pontus, but he never really encroached on Oceanus. Like another great pre-Olympian figure, his grandson Prometheus, Oceanus was seen as a benefactor of humankind. In some myths he and his mother Gaia were said to be the parents of Triptolemus, who brought

Above: A Roman mosaic depicting Oceanus. In Greek art Oceanus was usually portrayed as a creature that was half human and either half fish or half serpent. However, the Romans usually depicted him simply as a bearded man.

Oceanus's Family

Oceanus and his wife Tethys had 6,000 children—3,000 sons and 3,000 daughters—many of whom played important roles in Greek mythology. Oceanus's daughters, known as Oceanids, were nymphs who inhabited wells and streams. Often the gentle daughters of Oceanus married the more tempestuous sons of Pontus, god of the ocean, and produced famous offspring. One was Doris, who mated with Nereus, the Old Man of the Sea, to produce 50 sea nymphs known as Nereids, all renowned for their beauty. Among the best-known Nereids were Amphitrite, who became the wife of the Olympian sea god Poseidon, and Thetis, the mother of the hero Achilles. Another celebrated Nereid was Metis, the goddess of wisdom and the first wife of Zeus. According to one story, it was Metis who helped Zeus overthrow his father, Cronus. However, when Zeus learned that Metis was destined to bear a son who would become king of the gods, he swallowed her.

Other Oceanids married other sons of Pontus. Electra, for example, mated with Pontus's son Thaumas to produce both Iris, the goddess of the rainbow, and the Harpies, winged female monsters who tormented the blind king Phineus. Another Oceanid who produced a famous son was Clymene, who was the mother of the Titan Prometheus. Like Oceanus, Prometheus was a great benefactor of humankind, introducing fire to the world. A more malevolent descendant of Oceanus was the notorious murderer and sorceress Medea, wife of Jason. Medea was daughter of the Oceanid Eidyia.

While the daughters of Oceanus were usually nymphs, the sons of Oceanus were almost always identified with rivers. They included Scamander, god of the chief river of Troy; Istros, god of the river today known as the Danube; and Neilos of the Nile River in Egypt. Oceanus was also the father of Achelous, identified with the river of the same name that runs through northwestern Greece. The god Achelous is famous for his wrestling match with the Greek hero Heracles. One daughter of Oceanus who was identified with a river was Styx, who personified the chief river of the underworld.

Below: This painting by Joachim de Patinir (c. 1485–1524) depicts Charon the ferryman crossing the Styx River.

Right: A re-creation of the shield of Achilles by Antoine Chrysôthome Quatremère de Quincy (1755–1849). The river Oceanus is depicted around the rim of the shield, encircling the earth.

Demeter's gift of agriculture to the world. It is not difficult to see how the idea arose that agriculture came about as the result of a union between earth and water.

The ends of the world

As an all-encompassing world river, Oceanus was also thought of as an outer limit, a boundary beyond which lay only the unattainable and the mysterious. The ancient Greeks believed that the sun god Helios rode across the sky every day in a chariot, beginning his journey in the east, in Ethiopia. During the night, he was thought to travel back through the waters of Oceanus in either a cup or a golden bowl.

Oceanus also separated the realm of mortals from Hades, the land of the dead, and Elysium, the paradise reserved for the greatest heroes. Both were located on the banks of Oceanus, at the edge of the world. When the hero Odysseus visited Hades, he had to cross Oceanus to reach the grove of Persephone, where a secret entrance to the underworld was hidden.

Greek heroes were often presented with challenges that involved their having to reach Oceanus and even cross the river. For example, Heracles had to cross Oceanus in order to retrieve the golden apples of the Hesperides from their garden at the edge of the world. In order to do so he had to borrow Helios's golden bowl.

Oceanus was rarely seen as having a human form and personality in the way that Olympian deities such as Zeus and Poseidon were. However, he did appear in this guise in *Prometheus Bound*, a play by Aeschylus (525–456 BCE). In the play he advises his grandson not to do anything to aggravate Zeus, king of the gods.

Oceanus in art

In ancient art Oceanus was sometimes depicted as a creature that was half human and half animal. The lower half of his body was that of either a serpent or a fish. Although the upper half was basically humanlike in appearance, a bull's horn projected from the center of his forehead. The latter is significant because it marks Oceanus as a river god, rather than a deity of the sea. River gods were often described as having the head of a bull or possessing the ability to transform themselves into a bull. Oceanus often carried a snake in one hand, a symbol of the mysterious nature of his realm, and the contrasting figure of a dolphin in the other. In Roman times Oceanus was often represented as a bearded man, reclining and surrounded by his many offspring.

There were few cults dedicated to the worship of Oceanus. However, Alexander the Great (356–323 BCE) is said to have set up altars to him and Oceanus's wife Tethys at the delta of the Indus River. Also, the rivers and springs that were his offspring were the objects of worship in local cults throughout the Greek world.

ANTHONY BULLOCH

Bibliography

Hesiod, and M. L. West, trans. *Theogony; and Works and Days.* New York: Oxford University Press, 1999.

SEE ALSO: Gaia; Helios; Heracles; Nymphs; Prometheus.

ODIN

Odin was the chief Norse deity and the god of battle, poetry, magic, and wisdom. He was a highly complex figure of many attributes and guises, whose role in a number of significant myths was to seek out wisdom. The Norse believed that this knowledge would enable him to determine the time and place of Ragnarok, the final confrontation between the gods and the giants. Odin, who could predict the future, knew that he and the other gods were doomed to fall at this battle. While he was all-knowing, he was never all-powerful, and a sense of unreliability and even duplicity surrounded him.

Odin's father was Bor and his mother was Bestla. The pair were two of the first giants. Bor was the son of Búri, the giant who was licked into form from primordial ice by the primeval cow Audhumla; Bestla was a descendant of Ymir, the very first giant who was formed by the mingling of ice and fire in the mythical region of Ginnungagap, a yawning void that was the equivalent of the Greek Chaos. Odin's wife was Frigga, queen of the Norse goddesses, called the Ásynjur, who took an interest in mortals as the protector of marriage and the home. Despite his association with the giants, Odin was regarded as the head of the Aesir, the dominant group of Norse gods. Most sources agree that he was the father of three major deities: the beautiful and just Balder; Thor, god of thunder; and Váli, who would avenge the killing of Balder. Icelandic scholar Snorri Sturluson (1179–1241),

however, described Odin as Alfadur ("all-father"), and maintained that he also fathered five more of the Aesir: Bragi, god of poetry and eloquence; Heimdall, watchman of the gods; the blind god Höd, who unwittingly killed Balder; the ancient god of justice, Tyr; and Vídar, who would avenge Odin's death at Ragnarok.

One myth that emphasizes Odin's role as the chief god describes the drastic measures the Aesir undertook to protect themselves against the three terrible children of Loki, the trickster god. These offspring, produced from Loki's union with the giantess Angrboda, were the wolf Fenrir, the serpent Jörmungand, and half-alive half-decayed Hel. Odin ordered a group of gods to journey to Jotunheim, the land of the giants, to seize the three monsters and take them back to Asgard, the home of the gods. There, Odin hurled Jörmungand into the ocean surrounding Midgard, the world of humans. He next threw Hel into the underworld, where she presided as the goddess of death. Finally, Odin arranged for the wolf Fenrir to be bound by unbreakable chains. In this he was aided by Tyr, who allowed his hand to be bitten off while the gods fettered the animal.

A god of many attributes

Beside describing Odin as the most important of all the Norse gods, Snorri gave a detailed description of Odin's diverse qualities and attributes. Odin was the cleverest of all the gods. He spoke so cunningly that everyone who heard him believed his words. His manner and appearance could be pleasant and uplifting, but when he went to battle he was a deadly warrior who could make his enemies deaf, blind, or paralyzed with fear while inspiring his own soldiers to frenzied acts of violence. Odin had the ability to change his shape at will—Snorri described how the god would appear to be sleeping, while in the form of a fish, snake, or bird he could journey to distant places. He had the ability to calm stormy seas, change the direction of the wind, and put out fires. He was also skilled in all forms of magic, which enabled him to discover hidden treasure no matter where it was buried, to bring misfortune and death on humans, and to predict the future. These different abilities help explain the great number of names the Norse had for Odin—more than 150 in total—including Valfödr

Above: The Norse god Odin is often represented in art accompanied by symbolic creatures. In this illustration taken from a 16th-century manuscript, his two ravens, Hugin (thought) and Munin (memory), perch upon his shoulders.

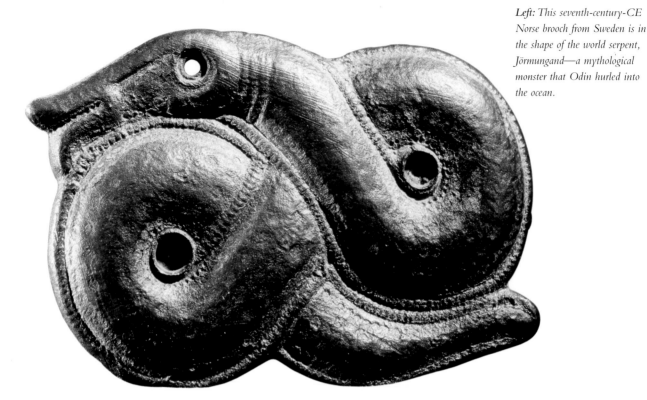

Left: This seventh-century-CE Norse brooch from Sweden is in the shape of the world serpent, Jörmungand—a mythological monster that Odin hurled into the ocean.

("father of the slain"), Hangagud ("god of the hanged"), and Haptagud ("god of the bound").

The most familiar representation of Odin portrayed him as an old, one-eyed man wearing a cloak and a broad-brimmed hat. It is in this form, for example, that the god appears in the *Völsunga Saga,* a 13th-century Icelandic narrative that recounts the story of the heroic warrior Sigmund and his son Sigurd, and in the *Gesta Danorum* (History of the Danes) by Danish historian Saxo Grammaticus (c.1150–after 1216), in a story in which Odin appears to King Harald War-tooth. This standard image of Odin also describes him with an extensive array of divine possessions. Some of these were Odin's ship, Skídbladnir, which he could roll up and fit into his pocket; his spear Gungnir, which could determine the outcome of a battle by the direction it took when thrown; and his gold ring Draupnir, from which nine new rings dropped every ninth night. Some of the god's most important possessions were animals, particularly the eight-legged horse Sleipnir (see box, page 1030), but also the two ravens Hugin ("thought") and Munin ("memory"), who flew far and wide collecting news for Odin, and the two wolves, Freki and Geri, to whom Odin fed leftovers from his feasts.

Odin's best-known possession, however, was his hall Valhalla, where he welcomed warriors who had died a heroic death on the battlefield. The Norse believed that by day these dead warriors fought each other in battles, while each night they feasted in Valhalla, eating a roasted boar that never ran out of meat and drinking mead (an alcoholic drink made from honey) produced by a goat that never ran dry. The purpose behind Odin's hospitality was to assemble a great army of men to join the gods at Ragnarok in their final confrontation with the giants and their allies. While marshaling this army, Odin was assisted by the Valkyries, female spirits who flew over battlefields and selected dead warriors to go to Valhalla. One of the most famous Valkyries in Norse myth was Brynhild, who disobeyed Odin by granting a fallen warrior life instead of leading him to the god's hall. As punishment, Odin made Brynhild marry a mortal and so become mortal herself.

The creation of the world

The importance of Odin in Norse mythology can be seen from his role in the story of the creation of the world. Odin's two brothers were Vili and Vé. Over time the three siblings grew to hate the first giant Ymir, so they attacked and killed him. So much blood flowed from Ymir's wounds that all the other giants were drowned—except for Bergelmir and his wife, who made a boat out of a hollowed tree trunk and sailed away to found a new race of giants. Odin and his brothers created the cosmos out of Ymir's body. They made the earth from his flesh and the mountains from his unbroken bones, while the giant's broken bones and teeth became rocks and boulders. They made lakes, seas, and oceans from his blood, and then made the sky from his skull. Odin, Vili, and Vé then separated the cosmos into different realms: Jotunheim, the home of the giants; Midgard, the home of people; and Asgard, the home of the gods. Odin then took one of the giantesses from Jotunheim, called Night, and her son Day, and gave each of them a chariot with which they would ride around the world bringing successive periods of light and darkness.

Snorri also attributed to Odin and his brothers the creation of the first man and woman, although this account is at odds with other sources, such as the anonymous poem *Völuspá*. According to Snorri, one day Odin, Vili, and Vé were wandering over the lands that they had created when they came across two fallen trees, one an ash, the other an elm. The three gods made the ash tree into the first man,

Ask, and the elm into the first woman, Embla. Odin gave them the breath of life, Vili gave them intelligence and emotions, and Vé gave them sight and hearing.

The quest for wisdom

Three of the most important myths concerning Odin portrayed him in a quest for wisdom of some sort—whether it was knowledge of the future, of runes (letters), or of poetry. In one story that explained Odin's disfigurement, the god surrendered one of his eyes so that he might drink from the spring of Mímir. The spring, which ran under one of the roots of the world tree Yggdrasil, gave whoever drank from it the power of prophecy. The name Mímir also occurred in another story, this time as the wisest member of the Aesir who was sent as

Odin, God of Battle

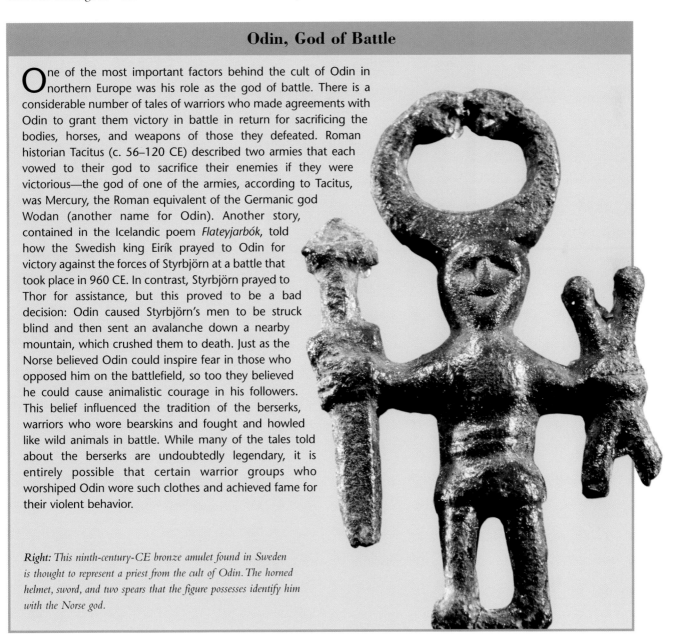

One of the most important factors behind the cult of Odin in northern Europe was his role as the god of battle. There is a considerable number of tales of warriors who made agreements with Odin to grant them victory in battle in return for sacrificing the bodies, horses, and weapons of those they defeated. Roman historian Tacitus (c. 56–120 CE) described two armies that each vowed to their god to sacrifice their enemies if they were victorious—the god of one of the armies, according to Tacitus, was Mercury, the Roman equivalent of the Germanic god Wodan (another name for Odin). Another story, contained in the Icelandic poem *Flateyjarbók*, told how the Swedish king Eirík prayed to Odin for victory against the forces of Styrbjörn at a battle that took place in 960 CE. In contrast, Styrbjörn prayed to Thor for assistance, but this proved to be a bad decision: Odin caused Styrbjörn's men to be struck blind and then sent an avalanche down a nearby mountain, which crushed them to death. Just as the Norse believed Odin could inspire fear in those who opposed him on the battlefield, so too they believed he could cause animalistic courage in his followers. This belief influenced the tradition of the berserks, warriors who wore bearskins and fought and howled like wild animals in battle. While many of the tales told about the berserks are undoubtedly legendary, it is entirely possible that certain warrior groups who worshiped Odin wore such clothes and achieved fame for their violent behavior.

Right: This ninth-century-CE bronze amulet found in Sweden is thought to represent a priest from the cult of Odin. The horned helmet, sword, and two spears that the figure possesses identify him with the Norse god.

a hostage to the rival group of gods, the Vanir. When the Vanir decapitated Mímir and sent his head back to the Aesir, Odin used magic to restore it to life. He then consulted Mímir's head, which was able to foretell the future, on any matter that concerned him.

Another, more elaborate myth relates how Odin gave poetic inspiration and wisdom to gods and humans. The origins of the myth lie with the truce between the Aesir and the Vanir, which was sealed when members of both groups spit into a jar. The combined spit formed an exceptionally wise being called Kvasir, who was subsequently murdered by two dwarfs, Fjaler and Galar. The

dwarfs mixed Kvasir's blood with honey to brew a mead that gave whoever drank it great wisdom and poetic ability. The mead then passed into the hands of a giant, Suttung, who took it as *weregild* (compensation for murder) for Fjaler and Galar's killing of his father. At this point Odin decided to steal the mead, which Suttung had hidden inside a mountain, guarded by his daughter Gunnlöd. Odin, who traveled in disguise under the name Bolverk ("evil work"), offered his services to Suttung's brother Baugi. He helped the giant harvest his crops on the condition that Baugi assist him in having one sip of his brother's mead, but when Odin had performed his half of

Right: This picture depicts Odin and Brynhild, one of the Valkyries—female figures who selected which of the battle-dead went to Valhalla.

the deal, Suttung refused his brother's request. Odin then persuaded Baugi secretly to drill a small hole into the mountain where the mead was kept. The god transformed himself into a snake and crawled through the hole until he came across Gunnlöd, whom he seduced. Odin slept with the giant's daughter for three nights, each night coaxing her into allowing him a sip from the mead. Three sips was all the god needed to drink of the precious liquid. He then changed into an eagle and flew back to Asgard. Suttung, who by now had discovered Odin's trick, turned himself into an eagle, too, and flew after the god. Odin made it back to the realm of the gods just in time, although in the version told by Snorri, the god spilled some of the mead along the way: it fell on Midgard, the world of humans, and introduced poetry to the world.

Odin's suffering

The third myth involving Odin in a quest for knowledge is one of the most obscure and also one of the most ambiguous. The story, the only surviving reference of which comes in the poem *Hávamál*, part of a 12th-century Icelandic collection of poems, named the Codex Regius, tells how Odin hung on a "wind-swept tree/nine entire nights/wounded with a spear." At the end of this time Odin was able to bend down from the tree, which in all likelihood was Yggdrasil, and lift up the magical runes that brought great knowledge. These runes gave him, among other things, the power to heal, to speak to people who had been hanged, to predict and prevent evil plans, to put out fires, to calm stormy seas, and to seduce his listeners. There are various interpretations of the myth. First, scholars have drawn parallels between Odin's act and that of shamans of central Asia who underwent near-death experiences to have visions and enhance their wisdom and their ability to predict the future. This similarity could be the result of rituals common to both ancient Scandinavian and central Asian cultures. On the other hand it could reflect the movement of Germanic peoples from central Asia to northern Europe in the centuries after the birth of Christ—some scholars believe that the name of the Aesir could be derived from that of one such people, the As or Alans. Second, many people have compared Odin's hanging on the tree to Christ's crucifixion on the cross. Both Odin and Christ sacrifice themselves voluntarily, both are pierced by a spear, and both

Gods and History

Above: This seventh-century-CE Norse helmet was discovered in a boat grave in Sweden. Norse peoples believed that boats carried the souls of the dead to their final resting place.

Euhemerism is a way of interpreting myths as part of history—for example, by asserting that a particular god was originally a real hero whom later generations elevated to a divine position. Christian writers often used euhemerism as a means of explaining the pagan myths they encountered. Such attempts are evident from two of the most important sources for Norse myths: Snorri Sturluson and Saxo Grammaticus. Snorri wrote that the Aesir were originally a group of people from western Asia. They lived in the city of Asgard, and their chief was a fearsome warrior called Odin. According to Snorri, Odin led his people out of Asia and traveled north, where his sons established kingdoms. Saxo's account is more detailed still. He wrote of a man named Odin who lived in Uppsala in Sweden and was wrongly worshiped as a god. His followers fashioned a golden statue of him, but Odin's wife, Frigga, persuaded one of her servants—with whom she was having an affair—to strip the statue of its gold. When he discovered his wife's two crimes, Odin went into exile. His place was filled by the sorcerer Mithotyn, who, like Odin, claimed to be divine. After some time, however, Odin returned, ordering that Mithotyn and other sorcerers like him be cast out of the country.

return to life. Some scholars suggest that the writer of *Hávamál* was influenced by the story of the crucifixion; others believe the poem was composed before Christianity reached Scandinavia and argue that the elements of the myth are consistent with pagan traditions.

The limits of knowledge

While Odin was regarded as all-wise, he was not all-powerful: his wisdom and ability to predict the future gave him, the Norse believed, the knowledge of his and the other gods' eventual downfall at Ragnarok. This combination of wisdom and impotence is a feature of the myth of Balder, Odin's son who was killed by Loki's treachery. When Balder fell, Odin alone understood the implications of his death—premonitions had come to him in dreams, and he knew that the death represented another step toward the destruction of Asgard. After Balder's demise, Hermód, messenger of the gods, rode down into Hel to try to bring the god back. Hel, however, would not let Balder return unless all things on earth wept for him. Frigga, Balder's mother, entreated the plants and animals to carry out Hel's wish. All did so except Loki,

who, in the form of an old woman, refused to cry for the dead god. The message underlying the myth is that Odin, even though he was the god of the dead, was unable to bring his own son back to life. Just as he was powerless to revive Balder, so too would he be powerless to prevent his own death and those of the other gods at Ragnarok.

In the minds of the Norse, the limits of Odin's power were linked to the god's reputation for treachery and duplicity. In a number of myths Odin promises help to mortals, but takes away his support at crucial moments. In the myth of Sigmund the Völsung, for instance, Odin supported the hero after he proved his worthiness by drawing out a sword that the god had plunged into a tree; but after Sigmund had won many victories, Odin appeared during a battle and broke the same sword with his spear, making the hero easy prey for his enemies, who killed him. Another story concerned King Harald War-tooth of Denmark. Odin appeared to the king and promised to support him if he sacrificed all his fallen enemies to the god. The king agreed, but years later Odin reappeared, stirred up enmity between Harald and his ally, King Hring, and then threw Harald from his own chariot,

Sleipnir, Odin's Horse

Odin's eight-legged horse Sleipnir was one of his most important possessions. The animal features on stone carvings, such as three of the famous Gotland stones of Sweden. It also played a role in the myth of Sigurd the dragon slayer as the parent of Grani, the magical horse Odin helped the young Sigurd choose. The myth of Sleipnir's own birth involves the rebuilding of the walls of Asgard, which had been destroyed in the war between the Aesir and the Vanir. A giant offered to rebuild the walls for the gods in the space of one winter, but his price was marriage to the beautiful fertility goddess Freya, as well as possession of the sun and the moon. The gods accepted the offer, sure that it was impossible for the giant to meet his own deadline. However, they had not reckoned on the giant's magic stallion, Svadilfari, who proved such a help to the builder that before long he had nearly completed the walls. Loki saved Freya, the sun, and the moon: he transformed himself into a mare and distracted Svadilfari so that the giant was unable to complete the walls. The giant was then killed by Thor; Svadilfari, meantime, had mated with Loki, who gave birth to Sleipnir.

Right: This eighth-century-CE stone was discovered in Sweden. Odin is depicted riding his eight-legged horse Sleipnir toward Valhalla, a round-topped building carved on the top left of the stone.

Right: German composer Richard Wagner (1813–1883) arranged an operatic score that was inspired by the Odin myth. This illustration from a program for the opera, Siegfried, *depicts Wotan (another name for Odin) wearing a typical cloak and hat.*

causing the king to die by falling on his own sword. Many of Odin's warrior supporters seem to have accepted that, as in the myths, their god would not grant them an infinite number of victories in battle and would, ultimately, let them down.

Odin's fickle nature is also present in his relationships with women. A familiar pastime for Odin was the seduction of attractive women, and he was repeatedly unfaithful to his wife, Frigga. In the poem *Hárbardsljód*, Odin boasts about his sexual triumphs to Thor and compares them in amount to the number of victories Thor has had on the battlefield. In various myths Odin was often portrayed as treacherous and unfaithful, but the ultimate treachery, the Norse believed, lay in the hands of fate, over which Odin had little control.

Odin and Thor

Multiple examples of Odin's treachery can be found in the poem *Hárbardsljód*, in which the god poses as the ferryman Hárbard ("gray beard"). He refuses to take Thor across a stretch of water in his boat and instead submits the thunder god to a tirade of insults. He tells the furious Thor that he is dressed like a beggar and describes him as faint-hearted; in an attempt to ridicule Thor's accomplishments he boasts of his own achievements, which involve using his magic powers and stirring up wars between kingdoms. Thor's achievements contrast with Odin's and emphasize the thunder god's role as the protector of gods and mortals. He tells Odin how he has killed giants such as Hrungnir and Thjazi. If it were not for his actions, he says, there would be huge numbers of giants in Midgard, and no people.

Another of Odin's insults in *Hárbardsljód* involves the remark, "Odin gets the noblemen who fall in battle/but Thor gets the kin of slaves." Scholars believe that this comment reflected the different levels of support for Odin and Thor among different social groups. Evidence exists to suggest that Odin was worshiped by rulers and warriors—weapons and skeletons of animals and people found in bogs in Scandinavia are believed to have been offered as battle sacrifices by his followers (see box, page 1027). In contrast, Thor's followers were ordinary men and women, who worshiped the thunder god both for his role as protector against evil and for his ability to control the weather—a crucial concern for fishing and farming

communities. The 11th-century German historian Adam of Bremen famously described a temple at Uppsala, Sweden, in which a statue of Thor was more prominent than that of Odin or that of Frey, the fertility god. One implication of this description is that, by the 11th century, Thor had become more important to some Scandinavian peoples than Odin. Another is that Thor was always the preeminent deity, but Odin's role as god of poetry led many Norse poets to exaggerate the importance of the one-eyed god.

ANDREW CAMPBELL

Bibliography

Lindow, John. *Norse Mythology: A Guide to the Gods, Heroes, Rituals, and Beliefs.* New York: Oxford University Press, 2002.

Simek, Rudolf, and Angela Hall, trans. *A Dictionary of Northern Mythology.* Rochester, NY: Boydell and Brewer, 1993.

SEE ALSO: Aesir; Balder; Creation Myths; Germanic Peoples; Hel; Kvasir; Loki; Sacrifice; Scandinavia; Sigurd; Thor; Valkyries; Vanir.

ODYSSEUS

Odysseus is most famous for his ten-year journey home from the Trojan War. The Greek hero was renowned for his intelligence and cunning, and his love for his family. He could also be arrogant, impulsive, and even cruel. In Roman mythology, Odysseus was called Ulysses.

Below: Romans called Odysseus by the name Ulysses. In his adventures, Ulysses often used a disguise to deceive an enemy. This first-century-BCE Roman coin depicts Ulysses disguised as a beggar.

In Greek myth, Odysseus was the son of Laertes, king of Ithaca, an island kingdom in northeastern Greece. Odysseus's mother was Anticleia, the granddaughter of Hermes, son of Zeus and the messenger of the gods. Odysseus married Penelope, and before he went to Troy, they had a son named Telemachus. According to some myths, after Odysseus returned from Troy they had two more sons, Poliporthes and Acusilaus. Odysseus also had several other children with women he met on his travels.

Did Odysseus really exist?

The main sources for the myth of Odysseus are the *Iliad* and the *Odyssey*, the two great surviving works of ancient Greek poet Homer (c. ninth–eighth century BCE). Many other ancient writers also wrote about Odysseus, including the great playwrights Sophocles (c. 496–406 BCE) and Euripides (c. 486–c. 406 BCE).

As in the case of many mythical heroes, the character of Odysseus could have been based on that of a real person. If this is true, the real Odysseus would have lived in the 13th century BCE, more than 3,000 years ago. Archaeologists believe that this was when the ancient city of Troy (in modern Turkey) was besieged. This battle is thought to have been behind the legend of the Trojan War. There is also an ancient tomb near Ithaca, which some archaeologists think could be Odysseus's tomb.

Odysseus's childhood

When Odysseus was born, his grandfather Autolycus came to visit and was asked to name the baby. He called the baby Odysseus, which can be translated as "victim of anger" or "the one people hate," suitable names for him in some ways.

As an older boy, Odysseus visited his grandfather and went hunting wild boar in a forest. When he was about to kill a fierce boar with his spear, it tore his leg open with one of its tusks. Odysseus had a long, thin scar on his left leg, above his knee, for the rest of his life.

Marriage and war

When he grew up, Odysseus became one of many princes and kings who went to Sparta and attempted to woo Helen, the most beautiful woman in the world. Helen's stepfather Tyndareos was afraid the suitors might fight, especially when Helen chose her husband. With typical cunning, Odysseus told Tyndareos that he had a plan to ensure that the suitors did not fight. He promised to tell Tyndareos the plan if he could marry his niece, Penelope. Tyndareos agreed. Odysseus told the king to make all the suitors swear an oath promising to respect Helen's choice, and to fight anyone who tried to part her from her husband. Helen chose Menelaus, and thanks to his plan, Odysseus also came home with a wife, Penelope.

When Trojan prince Paris fell in love with Helen and took her away to Troy, the suitors who had taken the oath were forced to go to Troy to win Helen back. Odysseus had taken the oath too, but he did not want to go; he loved his life in Ithaca with Penelope and their baby, Telemachus. Odysseus had also heard a prophecy that if he went to war, he would be away for many years.

When Odysseus did not come forward, Palamedes, a Greek prince renowned for his ingenuity, was sent to Ithaca to fetch him. Odysseus tried to avoid going to war by pretending to be insane, but Palamedes proved he was not. Palamedes took the baby Telemachus and threatened him with his sword (in some versions of the myth, Palamedes laid the baby in front of a plow Odysseus was driving). Odysseus immediately ran to save his son, thus demonstrating that his insanity was an act. Lacking any further excuses, Odysseus had no choice but to set off for Troy.

Odysseus at Troy

Odysseus was one of the greatest assets to the Greek army at Troy. He was a brave fighter and a brilliant strategist. He carried out a number of successful spying missions with his friend Diomedes. On one occasion, they captured a Trojan named Dolon and forced him to reveal where they could find King Rhesus of Thrace, who was helping the Trojans. They killed Dolon, then went and killed Rhesus and his men as they slept. Odysseus was so cunning that he was even able to sneak inside the walled city of Troy. Disguised as a beggar, he stole a statue of Athena called the Palladium.

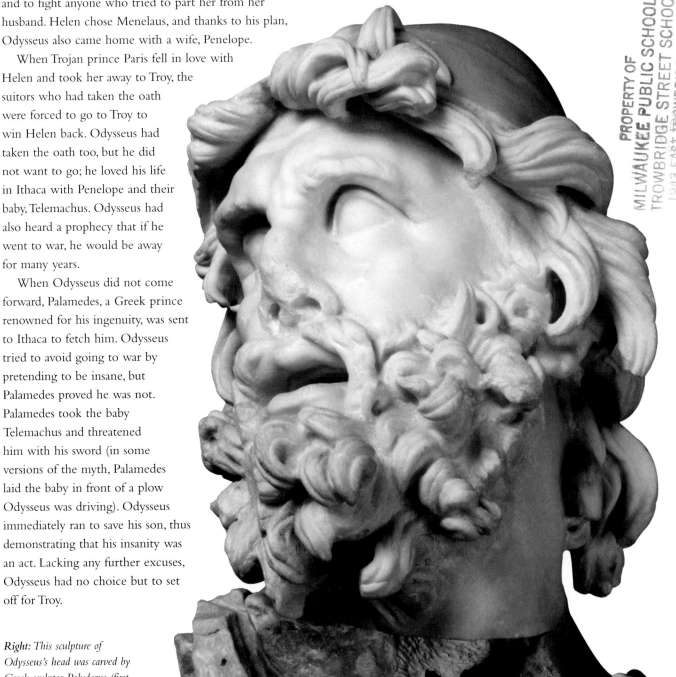

Right: This sculpture of Odysseus's head was carved by Greek sculptor Polydorus (first century BCE).

The Trojan Horse

The Greeks finally won the Trojan War by playing a trick on the Trojans. They built a huge wooden horse and left it outside Troy, then sailed away and hid at a nearby island. One Greek man, Sinon, was left to explain to the Trojans that the Greeks had retreated and gone home, leaving the horse as an offering to the goddess Athena. The Trojans took the horse into Troy. They did not realize that a band of Greek soldiers, including Odysseus, was hiding inside it. The hideaway Greeks climbed out of the horse and opened the gates of Troy to let in the rest of the Greek armies, who had sailed back to Troy, and the city was destroyed.

When she saw the horse being brought into Troy, Helen suspected something. She walked around it, calling out the names of Greek soldiers she knew, and imitated their wives' voices in the hope of making them call out if they were inside. A soldier named Anticlus nearly called out. To stop him, Odysseus held his hand over Anticlus's mouth for so long that he suffocated the man to death. This is one example of Odysseus's uncompromising nature.

Below: This 16th-century fresco by Italian painter Giulio Romano (c.1499–1546) depicts the construction of the Trojan horse.

At Troy, Odysseus also took his revenge on Palamedes. He had a Trojan captive write a fake letter, making it appear that Palamedes was spying for the Trojans. Then Odysseus buried some gold in Palamedes' tent. When the letter and the gold were discovered, Palamedes was accused of treachery and was stoned to death. According to some versions of the myth, Odysseus came up with the idea for the wooden horse, an invention that was decisive in the Greek victory at Troy.

The Odyssey

The Odyssey was the name given to Odysseus's travels after the Trojan War, as he made his way home from Troy with his men and ships and encountered a range of problems, including hostile peoples, monsters, and divine wrath.

First, Odysseus came to the land of the Ciconians. They had sided with Troy during the war. Odysseus and his men attacked them, killed many citizens, and stole food and

wine. Eventually the Ciconians called on neighboring peoples for help, and after a battle in which 70 of his men died, Odysseus fled.

Next Odysseus and his men came to the land of the Lotus-eaters, where some of Odysseus's men ate the fruit of the lotus plant. The lotus fruit made them forget their homes and families, and they wanted nothing more than to stay there and eat from the plants forever. Odysseus had to drag them back to the ships and chain them up. Finally, his fleet sailed on.

The Cyclops Polyphemus

Odysseus's most famous enemy was the Cyclops Polyphemus, a giant with one eye in the middle of his forehead. Odysseus and his crew arrived at Polyphemus's cave while he was out. Instead of taking some food and escaping, Odysseus wanted to wait and meet the monster. When Polyphemus returned with his flock of sheep, he

shut the men inside his cave and ate several of them for his supper, planning to eat the rest later.

Odysseus came up with a plan. First, he told Polyphemus his name was Nobody. Then he persuaded the monster to drink lots of wine. When the Cyclops was asleep, Odysseus and his men blinded the giant by driving a sharpened stake into his eye. Polyphemus called to his friends for help, but when he cried "Nobody has hurt me!" they ignored him. The next day, Odysseus and his men tied themselves under the Cyclops's sheep, and in this way escaped from the cave.

However, as he set sail, Odysseus could not resist taunting Polyphemus. He boasted about how he had escaped and revealed his real name. Polyphemus threw a rock at Odysseus in anger and missed. Finally, the Cyclops called on his father, the sea god Poseidon, to curse Odysseus and to cause him trouble on his journey home.

So near, and so far

Next, Odysseus visited Aeolus, the keeper of the winds. Aeolus welcomed the travelers. He gave Odysseus a bag containing all the winds so that he could sail wherever he wanted. Odysseus could return directly to Ithaca. As they approached the shore, Odysseus fell asleep. Hoping to find treasure, some of his men looked inside the bag Aeolus had

Above: This Roman mosaic depicts Odysseus and one of his men trapped in Polyphemus's cave. As part of his plan to escape the cave, Odysseus offers wine to the Cyclops in the hope of intoxicating him.

Who Was Homer?

Homer was a poet who lived around the 8th century BCE. He composed two great epic poems, the *Iliad* and the *Odyssey*. These poems were about the Trojan War, which, if it happened, took place in the 12th or 13th centuries BCE. In Homer's time, poets composed their work in their heads and recited it aloud. Homer's poems were eventually written down and passed on to later generations. The ancient Greeks who lived after Homer regarded him with great respect. Homer's poems were treasured and were central to Greek culture. According to legend, Homer was born in a Greek settlement on the coast of Asia Minor (modern Turkey), and was blind.

However, many modern experts think that poems attributed to Homer were actually written by more than one person and were probably changed and added to over time. Some people have even suggested that there was really no such person as Homer. We know so little about his period of history that the truth may never be discovered.

Right: In this fresco, Italian painter Alessandro Allori (1535–1607) depicts the meeting in Hades between Odysseus and the aged seer Tiresias.

given Odysseus. The winds escaped and blew up a storm, the ships were blown away from Ithaca, and Odysseus was lost again. He returned to Aeolus to ask for more help, but Aeolus was angry that his gift had been misused, and he sent him away.

Odysseus next stopped at the land of the Laestrygonians, a fierce cannibal tribe. While Odysseus moored his own ship outside the bay, the captains of his other ships decided to sail into the harbor. The Laestrygonians attacked the ships, pelting them with rocks. Trapped in the harbor, they could not escape. Only Odysseus's ship and crew survived.

Circe

Odysseus's ship then came to the island of Aeaea, home of the goddess Circe. Circe used her magic to turn some of Odysseus's men into pigs, but the god Hermes came to their rescue. He gave Odysseus a magic herb, moly, that would help him resist Circe's magic. When Circe met

Odysseus and realized she could not control him, she fell in love with him. She returned his men to their human forms and invited them all to stay.

Odysseus and his men stayed with Circe for a year. Before they left, Circe gave them directions to Hades, the land of the dead, where they could find the soul of Tiresias, a seer who would tell Odysseus his future. Odysseus reached Hades by sailing down the River of Ocean (Oceanus). Tiresias told him not to harm the cattle on Helios's island of Thrinacia, which he would soon visit. He also warned Odysseus that in Ithaca, his wife Penelope was being harassed by suitors who believed Odysseus was dead and wanted to marry her and take over the throne. Finally, Tiresias told Odysseus he would live to be old, and that death would come to him out of the sea. In Hades, Odysseus also met his mother, Anticleia, who had died while he was away, and Greek leader Agamemnon, who had been murdered by his wife on his return from Troy.

The Tomb of Odysseus

Some people believe that an ancient Greek tomb at Poros, on the island of Cephalonia, could be the grave of Odysseus. The tomb is a *tholos*, a dome-shaped underground chamber containing many graves. It dates from the Mycenaean period (1400–1100 BCE), when the events leading up to the Trojan War are thought to have occurred.

Cephalonia is the closest island to Ithaca, and since Homer does not mention it as a separate kingdom, some experts think Cephalonia might originally have been part of the kingdom of Ithaca. If this is true, it would make sense that Odysseus is buried there. *Tholos* tombs were often used to bury royalty, and the graves in the Poros tomb contained gold and jewelry, suggesting that the person who was buried there was very wealthy.

However, with such an old tomb, it is very hard to prove who was buried there. Even if it was Odysseus, his life was probably very different than that of the famous mythical hero.

Further trials

Next, Odysseus encountered the Sirens, beautiful but deadly bird-women. The Sirens sang a haunting melody that lured men toward the treacherous rocks where they lived. In this way, countless sailors had lost their lives. Wishing to hear the song, Odysseus followed Circe's advice and plugged his men's ears with wax, then told them to tie

Below: In this vase painting, Odysseus is tied tightly to the mast of his ship. Safely bound, he cannot succumb to the winged Sirens' enchanting songs as they circle him and his men.

him to the mast. When Odysseus's ship came near the Sirens and he heard their singing, he begged to be set free, but his men refused, and they passed the Sirens safely.

Odysseus then had to sail between Charybdis, a deadly whirlpool, and Scylla, a six-headed monster. Scylla and Charybdis were on opposite sides of the Straits of Messina, which separate Sicily and mainland Italy. Circe had told him the only way to survive would be to sail close to Scylla, who would snatch six of his men. Keeping this secret from his crew, Odysseus did as Circe had said and escaped. Six of his men paid with their lives.

Left: This illustration by the British artist H. J. Ford (1860–1941) depicts the encounter between Odysseus and Nausicaa. Although Nausicaa is surprised by the naked man, she rescues Odysseus and delivers him to her father, King Alcinous.

but with the help of other gods, Odysseus was washed ashore at Phaeacia, a land near Ithaca.

Odysseus was rescued by Nausicaa, the princess of Phaeacia, who took him to her father, King Alcinous. Alcinous threw a banquet for him, and at the table Odysseus revealed who he was and told everyone about his amazing adventures. The next day, a Phaeacian ship took him to Ithaca and left him on the shore. However, the goddess Athena, who had been protecting Odysseus, now told him he must disguise himself before going home. She warned him that Penelope's suitors—Ithacan nobles who had invaded Odysseus's home and, believing him to be dead, sought to marry his wife—would kill him unless he took them by surprise. After reuniting him with his son Telemachus, who was told about the plan, Athena made Odysseus look like an old beggar, and in this disguise he went home to his palace.

Almost 100 suitors had taken over the palace. They were eating Odysseus's food and drinking his wine while bullying Penelope and Telemachus. Penelope had run out of hope and decided to marry the suitor who was strong enough to string and fire Odysseus's old bow. The suitors failed, but Odysseus, still disguised, took the bow and fired it with ease. Then, with the help of an old swineherd, Eumaeus, a young cowherd, Philoetius, and the goddess Athena disguised as an old friend of Odysseus named Mentor, Odysseus and Telemachus killed all the suitors in a gruesome bloodbath. At first Penelope could not believe her husband had returned, but his old nursemaid, Eurycleia, knew him by his scar. When he was able to describe their marriage bed exactly, Penelope finally knew it was Odysseus.

Old age and death

Odysseus's travels were not yet over. The families of the slain suitors complained to King Neoptolemus of Epirus, and he ruled that Odysseus must be exiled. Odysseus eventually returned to Ithaca and lived to be an old man. Tiresias's prophecy about the death of Odysseus was fulfilled. Telegonus, the son of Odysseus and Circe, came to Ithaca to find his father. He came in peace, but when Odysseus confronted him, Telegonus did not recognize Odysseus and wounded him with his spear. The spear was tipped with a poisonous stingray spine, and Odysseus died.

Finally, Odysseus reached the island of Thrinacia, where the cattle and sheep of the sun god Helios were grazing. Because of Tiresias's warning, Odysseus was reluctant to land there, but his men were tired, so he said they could rest there for one night as long as they left the cattle alone. While Odysseus and his men were at Thrinacia, a storm blew up and they could not leave. They ran out of food, and one day, while Odysseus was busy praying for help, his men slaughtered some of the sacred cattle to eat. Helios begged Zeus to punish them, so when they set sail again, Zeus sent a thunderbolt to destroy the ship. The crew drowned, and only Odysseus survived. He drifted for many days until he came to the island of Ogygia, home of the nymph Calypso.

Calypso was lonely, and she was delighted to see Odysseus. She cared for him in every way she could. She also held him prisoner, keeping him on her island for seven years, though he longed to go home. Finally the gods agreed he must be set free. They sent Hermes to tell Calypso to let him go. Odysseus made a boat and set off. Poseidon still tried to stop him by sending another storm,

James Joyce's *Ulysses*

Irish writer James Joyce (1882–1941) is famous for his novel *Ulysses*, published in 1922. Joyce wanted to create a modern version of Homer's poem the *Odyssey*. Instead of a ten-year journey, Joyce made the action take place over the course of a single day, June 16, 1904, in Dublin. The hero, Leopold Bloom, represents Ulysses (or Odysseus) as he wanders around his city. Bloom's wife Molly stands for Penelope, and his friend's son, Stephen Dedalus, is Telemachus.

Each chapter in Joyce's *Ulysses* corresponds to an episode of Homer's poem. For example, Chapter 12, known as the Cyclops chapter, has several parallels with Homer's Cyclops myth. It is set in a dark Dublin bar, representing the Cyclops's cave, and Bloom, the hero, uses a fake name, as Odysseus does. At the end of the chapter, someone throws a biscuit at Bloom and misses, just as the Cyclops throws the errant rock at Odysseus.

Left: This photograph of Irish writer James Joyce was taken in 1938. The author of Ulysses *was visiting Zurich, Switzerland.*

A popular hero

Despite his shortcomings, Odysseus has always been regarded as a hero. The ancient Greeks admired his cunning and wit and saw him as a fine leader. Although he was merciless toward his enemies and could often be unnecessarily cruel, he always acted with courage. Odysseus's decisiveness during the Trojan War and on his travels averted many potential disasters.

Odysseus's adventures also contain many moral lessons. Whenever Odysseus is arrogant, boastful, or complacent, fate and the gods punish him. His adventures suggest that there is often a bad consequence for someone who carries out a bad deed. As well as being clever and brave, Odysseus sometimes makes mistakes or loses control, and he always suffers for it. Perhaps this is why Odysseus is such a well-loved character, even though his personality is often disagreeable. He is a kind of everyman: someone that is easy to identify with since he does his best in life's journey; he goes through ups and downs, and he has to struggle against his own weaknesses to survive.

The Odyssey as inspiration

Odysseus is most famous for his epic journey, which has now become part of modern speech. The word *odyssey* is used to describe any long journey, especially one that teaches someone a lot about themselves, whether it is a physical journey or an inner journey of self-discovery.

The *Odyssey*'s simple structure of disaster and recovery, the exciting monsters, and the universal theme of longing for home make the poem enduringly popular. The *Odyssey* has been translated and retold countless times in books, films, and literature. A famous example is Irish writer James Joyce's novel *Ulysses,* which is based on the *Odyssey.* The poem has also inspired more recent works such as *2001: A Space Odyssey* and the TV series *Star Trek: Voyager,* in which the crew of a spaceship encounters many monsters and strange peoples on their long journey home. Odysseus and his adventures have been depicted in many carvings, paintings and sculptures, from ancient Greek times to the present day.

ANNA CLAYBOURNE

Bibliography

Apollodorus, and Robin Hard, trans. *The Library of Greek Mythology.* New York: Oxford University Press, 1999.

Graves, Robert. *The Greek Myths.* New York: Penguin USA, 1993.

Homer, and Robert Fagles, trans. *The Iliad.* New York: Penguin USA, 2003.

Homer, and Robert Fagles, trans. *The Odyssey.* New York: Penguin USA, 1999.

SEE ALSO: Achilles; Agamemnon; Athena; Calypso; Circe; Cyclopes; Demigods and Heroes; Helen; Helios; Penelope; Poseidon; Tiresias; Zeus.

OEDIPUS

In Greek mythology Oedipus was the son of Laius, King of Thebes, and Jocasta, who is also known as Epicasta. He is renowned as a man who endured a life that was full of misfortune, during which he unwittingly killed his father and married his mother.

The oldest version of the Oedipus myth appears in Homer's (c. ninth–eighth century BCE) epic poems the *Iliad* and the *Odyssey*. Homer's version of the myth is different from later versions found in fifth-century-BCE Greek tragedies. The most famous of these tragedies were written by Sophocles (c. 496–406 BCE)—*Oedipus the King* and *Oedipus at Colonus*—and by Aeschylus (525–456 BCE)—*The Seven Against Thebes*. Some scholars speculate that tragedians changed the myth to make it more politically and socially relevant to contemporary Greek society. The plague mentioned in the opening of *Oedipus the King*, for example, is thought to refer to a great plague that affected Athens in 430 BCE. Scholars also suggest that in *Oedipus at Colonus*, King Theseus's sympathy for Oedipus, who had been exiled from Thebes, offers an insight into how democratic Athens was during this period.

Homer's Oedipus

According to Homer, Oedipus was a prince of the house of Cadmus in Thebes. Before his birth, his father, King Laius, had been warned by a prophet that he would be killed by his son, so he ordered a herdsman to abandon the baby Oedipus in the woods. (In many ancient cultures, "exposure" was used as a form of birth control. Unwanted newborn babies were abandoned to die or to be picked up by a passerby. If the baby was adopted, he or she might be raised in a family or become a slave.) Oedipus was adopted by King Polybus and Queen Periboea of Corinth and lived peacefully until he unwittingly killed his real father during a chance encounter on the road to Thebes. Oedipus then married the widow of Laius, who was his own mother.

In the *Odyssey*, Homer names the queen Epicasta. When the incestuous marriage comes to light, Epicasta kills herself and Oedipus is cursed by being pursued by the Erinyes (Furies). Unlike in later versions of the myth, Oedipus did not gouge out his eyes and was not exiled from Thebes. Instead, he continued to rule Thebes and married again. Finally, he died a hero in battle, and at his funeral, games were held in his honor.

Other versions of the myth

Later versions of the Oedipus myth give more details in the story. They recount that Laius, king of Thebes, married Jocasta, daughter of Menoeceus, uniting two branches of the royal house of Thebes. Laius became anxious about the couple's difficulty in producing a child and consulted the oracle at Delphi. The oracle warned Laius not to have a son because that son was fated to kill his father. To prevent the prophecy from being fulfilled, Laius avoided making love to women, including his wife. (In one version of the myth, Laius kidnapped Chrysippus, the son of King Pelops of Pisa, to be his companion. Since the Thebans did not reprimand Laius for this action, the gods sent the Sphinx, a winged creature with a woman's head and a lion's body, to punish them.) However, Laius did not tell his wife why he was avoiding her, which made Jocasta unhappy, so she plotted to seduce her husband. One night, when he was drunk, Jocasta succeeded and became pregnant. Jocasta knew nothing of the prophecy. She was therefore horrified when the fearful Laius took away their healthy baby and abandoned the boy. In an effort to ensure that the baby was not adopted, Laius pierced his ankles with brooches or spikes. Then the king instructed a herdsman to leave the baby on Mount Cithaeron, between Boeotia and Attica. There, the baby was either found by servants of King Polybus of Corinth or given to them by the herdsman. The servants took the baby to Corinth, where Polybus's wife, Queen Periboea, healed the baby's ankles and adopted him. She named him Oedipus, which means "swollen feet" in ancient Greek. In a variation of the myth, Oedipus was born to Laius and his first wife; Jocasta was Laius's second wife. As a baby Oedipus was put into a chest and tossed

into the sea. The chest floated to Sicyon and was discovered by Polybus, who was king of Sicyon. In this version, Oedipus also eventually married Jocasta, his stepmother.

Oedipus grew up as prince and heir to the throne of Corinth, but his companions taunted him. They insisted that Oedipus could not be Polybus's son because the king was so mild and Oedipus was so aggressive. Oedipus approached the queen about the rumor, but she told him nothing of his adoption. The young man went to Delphi to consult the oracle about his parentage. The oracle advised Oedipus not to return to his native land. If he did, the oracle warned him, he would murder his father and sleep with his mother. Believing that the oracle was referring to Polybus and Periboea, Oedipus did not return to Corinth.

Patricide

Oedipus traveled in another direction, toward Daulis. On his way, on a narrow road, Oedipus encountered a chariot driven by two men, one of whom, unknown to Oedipus,

Above: This painting by an anonymous 17th-century artist depicts the discovery of Oedipus by servants of King Polybus after the baby had been abandoned on Mount Cithaeron.

was his natural father, Laius. Laius was going to consult the oracle at Delphi about how to rid Thebes of the Sphinx that was terrorizing the city. In another version of the myth, Laius was visiting the oracle because he had witnessed omens that foretold his death, and he wanted to discover if they were true. When father and son met on the narrow road, the king's herald Polyphontes ordered Oedipus to give way. According to some versions, Oedipus hesitated, so the herald killed one of his horses; in another the king urged his horses forward and a wheel bruised one of Oedipus's feet. In both stories Oedipus killed the herald with his spear, then dragged Laius from the chariot and killed him.

King Damasistratus of the nearby city of Plataea presided over Laius's funeral. Jocasta's brother and Oedipus's uncle, Creon, became regent in Thebes. During his rule the

Sphinx continued to terrorize Boeotia. It destroyed the fields around Thebes and killed anyone who failed to give the correct answer to a riddle, which it had learned from the Muses. The riddle is well known today: "What creature walks on all fours in the morning, two legs at noon, and three legs in the evening?" Some tragedians claimed that the Sphinx also had a second riddle: "There are two sisters. One gives birth to the other, then that one gives birth to the first. Who are they?" The answer to the second riddle is Night and Day, which are both feminine nouns.

In ancient Greece there were two versions of how the Sphinx forced the Thebans to guess its riddles. In one the monster came to the city each day to ask its riddle. Each time it was answered incorrectly, it devoured one of the citizens. In other versions of the story it perches on top of the citadel, or by the side of the road, and prevents travelers from passing if they provide an incorrect answer. The Thebans were desperate to escape the curse. There are stories that they gathered in the Agora (a marketplace found in most ancient Greek cities) to debate possible answers to the riddle, but without success. According to one version of the myth, Creon's own son Haemon was eaten by the Sphinx. However, Haemon also appears in the play *Antigone,* which is set after the death of the Sphinx.

Whether Creon was grief-stricken at the loss of his son or was simply a frustrated ruler, he promised the kingdom

Below: This third-century-BCE marble relief depicts Oedipus dragging Laius from his chariot to kill him.

of Thebes and the hand of his sister, Jocasta, to the person who could rid Thebes of the Sphinx. Many men came to try, but they all failed and were killed by the monster. News of the proclamation eventually reached Oedipus, and he headed for Thebes, where he met the Sphinx. Oedipus solved the riddle. The answer was a man. As an infant, humans are four-footed, crawling on their arms and legs; as adults they go on two feet; when they are elderly they walk using a cane like a third leg. On hearing the right answer, the Sphinx threw itself to its death.

Oedipus was welcomed into Thebes as a hero. He was crowned king and offered the hand of the widowed queen. Oedipus thus unwittingly married his mother. According to Sophocles' play *Oedipus the King,* when Oedipus became king he decreed that the murderer of Laius was to be found and brought to justice, and that he or she would be killed or banished from the kingdom.

Incest

According to some accounts Oedipus and Jocasta had four children: Eteocles, Polyneices, Antigone, and Ismene. Other accounts attribute other wives to the hero, possibly to overcome audiences' distaste at the idea of incest between a mother and son. In these accounts Euryganeia, the second wife of Oedipus, was sometimes credited as the mother of Eteocles, Polyneices, Antigone, and Ismene. Jocasta was childless, or their children were two obscure mythological characters called Phrastor and Laonytus. In some versions of the myth Oedipus married again after Euryganeia, to a

The Greek Sphinx

According to different myths, the Greek Sphinx was the female offspring of the monster Typhon and the snake-woman monster Echidna, or of the two-headed hound Orthus and the fire-breathing she-goat monster Chimaera. Her sister was the Nemean Lion, a murderous beast that Heracles had to kill for his first labor. Hera, the goddess of marriage, sent the Sphinx to terrorize Thebes because she held the Thebans accountable for Oedipus's marriage to his mother. Although Homer and tragedians agree that Oedipus solved the Sphinx's riddle, there are various accounts of how the Sphinx met her death. The most common version states that the Sphinx threw herself from a great height onto rocks, but another version claims that Oedipus pushed the Sphinx to her death. While both accounts are equally dramatic, the second undermines the exercise of solving the riddle and is not traditional.

Right: Oedipus confronts the Sphinx in this painting by French artist Gustave Moreau (1826–1898). The Sphinx was a monster with a woman's head, eagle's wings, and lion's body.

princess named Astymedusa. Some scholars speculate that the extra marriages were intended to avoid any implication that the Theban royal family was incestuous.

When Oedipus and Jocasta's children were reaching adulthood, a plague came upon the city. Eventually the plague became so bad that the Thebans consulted the blind seer Tiresias. Tiresias declared that the pestilence would cease if a descendent of the founders of Thebes died voluntarily to save the city. Menoeceus, father of Jocasta, threw himself to his death from the walls of the city. The plague ceased but Tiresias now said that although the gods were content with the death of Menoeceus, they had originally referred to another man. Tiresias told Jocasta that this man was Oedipus, and when she told her husband, he arrogantly refused to believe her. Around this time, however, Oedipus received a letter from his adoptive mother, Queen Periboea of Corinth. The letter, written following the death of King Polybus, revealed Oedipus's true identity. He was Jocasta's son and Laius's murderer. Menoetes, the herdsman who had exposed Oedipus when he was a baby, also identified him by the scars on his feet and ankles as the son of Laius. On hearing the news, Jocasta either hanged herself or killed herself with a sword, while Oedipus blinded himself with brooches that he tore from

Jocasta's robes. Following the sentence he himself had decreed for the murderer of Laius, Oedipus went into exile, accompanied by his daughter Antigone. Before leaving, Oedipus handed the kingdom of Thebes to his sons Polyneices and Eteocles. Some versions of the myth claim that his sons imprisoned him before he could leave Thebes, hoping that his disgrace might be forgotten. Oedipus cursed his sons so that they would never agree between them who should become the next king of Thebes.

The Oedipus Complex

Sigmund Freud (1856–1939) was a psychologist who is regarded as the father of psychoanalysis by psychologists today. He used Oedipus's name as shorthand for instances when his patients experienced a sexual attraction to their parents; his interpretation of the myth is renowned. Freud's theory of the Oedipus complex centers around the idea that between the ages of 3 and 5 a child experiences feelings of attraction toward the parent of the opposite sex. At the same time, the child experiences a feeling of rivalry with the parent of the same sex. Freud argued that these issues were part of normal human development. Modern psychologists argue that Freud's theory is not correct and interpret the Oedipus myth differently; they explain the relationship between Oedipus and his parents in terms of resentment of parental authority, not sexual rivalry.

Below: This illustration from de Claris Mulieribus, *by Italian author Giovanni Boccaccio (1313–1375), depicts different stages of the Oedipus myth. The woman stabbing herself is Oedipus's mother Jocasta, who cannot bear the fact that she has married her son.*

Polyneices and Eteocles tried to avoid the curse by agreeing that they should rule Thebes alternately for a year at a time. This agreement did not last long, however: Eteocles seized power and refused to share the throne with his brother.

Meanwhile, Oedipus had taken refuge at Colonus in Attica, where he was welcomed by King Theseus of Athens. While he was in Colonus, the disagreement between his sons worsened and war approached. Before conflict broke out, an oracle stated that the victor would be allied with Oedipus. Creon came to Oedipus on behalf of Eteocles and attempted to persuade him to return to Thebes. When Oedipus refused, Creon endeavored to take him there by force. Theseus intervened in time to save Oedipus, who remained in Colonus.

Aided by King Adrastus of Argos, Polyneices raised an army to march against his younger brother, who had banished Polyneices from Thebes and now controlled the city. Polyneices went to his exiled father at Colonus and asked for his support. Oedipus responded to the request by issuing another curse, in which he doomed his sons to kill each other.

The Thebans prepared for war by taking their treasures out of the city. Soon after, allies of Polyneices known as

Above: This painting by French artist Ernest Hillemacher (1818–1887) shows Antigone guiding her blind father, Oedipus. In some versions of the myth, Oedipus blinds himself after discovering that he has killed his father and married his mother.

the Seven Against Thebes attacked the city. Polyneices' forces were defeated, Oedipus's sons killed each other in battle, and Creon came to power again. Oedipus's daughter Ismene also perished during the war. She was killed in bed by Tydeus, king of Argos, while she lay with her lover Theoclymenus.

After the war King Creon decreed that the body of Polyneices be left on the battlefield to rot. In ancient Greece, this was an undignified end for fallen soldiers. When Creon's niece Antigone learned of her brother's death and Creon's edict, she insisted that Polyneices be buried. When Creon discovered her disobedience, he imprisoned her for failing to follow his decree. Antigone killed herself in captivity. Ten years later, sons of the seven allies of Polyneices, known as the Epigoni, captured Thebes to avenge the death of their fathers.

Shortly after meeting with Polyneices, Oedipus died. Some versions of the myth say that he died at Colonus, others say that it was Thebes. Again, accounts differ as to whether he died of natural causes or killed himself. Although Oedipus was an exile and an outcast in most versions of the myth, his grave was regarded with reverence by ancient Greeks because of a prophecy which said that any land containing his tomb would be blessed by the gods.

LYN GREEN

Bibliography

Bulfinch, Thomas. *Bulfinch's Mythology*. New York: Modern Library, 1998.

Homer, and Robert Fagles, trans. *The Iliad*. New York: Penguin USA, 2003.

Homer, and Robert Fagles, trans. *The Odyssey*. New York: Penguin USA, 1999.

Howatson, M. C., and Ian Chilvers. *Concise Oxford Companion to Classical Literature*. New York: Oxford University Press, 1993.

SEE ALSO: Antigone; Cadmus; Furies; Hera; Heracles; Muses; Sphinx; Theseus; Tiresias.

OLMECS

Historians believe that the Olmecs developed the first major civilization in Mesoamerica (Central America and Mexico) between about 1500 and 400 BCE. They left a cultural legacy for subsequent peoples that included the notion of kingship, trade routes, and symbolic art and architecture. Olmec religion also had a profound influence on the beliefs and practices of other civilizations of the region, from the Maya to the Aztec.

Below: This Olmec head was unearthed by archaeologists at La Venta, an island in the Tonalá River near the Gulf Coast in western Tabasco, Mexico.

The Olmecs lived in the humid lowlands of southern Mexico along the Gulf Coast, in the present-day states of Tabasco and Veracruz. They were primarily an agricultural, corn-growing people whose prosperity derived from the natural resources of their area of settlement, particularly its fertile soils and heavy rainfall. Olmec sites, such as those discovered at San Lorenzo and La Venta, include pyramids, underground drainage systems, and enormous stone sculptures of heads, variously interpreted as depictions of sacred ancestors, deities, or rulers. The sculptures were carved from basalt rock, hewn from the Tuxtla Mountains—which, in the case of San Lorenzo, lay 50 miles (80 km) away—and transported by river to the settlements. This great undertaking suggests both the extent of social control wielded by Olmec rulers and the vast number of human laborers at their disposal.

The Olmecs also had a highly developed trading network that extended over much of Mesoamerica. They imported from highland Mexico and Guatemala goods such as obsidian, which they used for blades and darts. Other minerals, such as jade and serpentine that were used to make ceremonial artworks, were traded from as far away as Costa Rica. These trade routes allowed Olmec ideas about ritual, religion, and kingship to spread to other peoples. Olmec artifacts have been discovered across an area more than 20 times larger than the civilization's Gulf Coast heartland, suggesting the extent of their influence on other peoples and subsequent civilizations.

Like most aspects of Olmec civilization, little is known for certain about Olmec mythology—in the almost complete absence of written records, knowledge of this remarkable people's beliefs is based largely on interpretation and speculation. The decline of Olmec civilization is also mysterious. Evidence suggests that the settlement at San Lorenzo was destroyed around 900 BCE, possibly by foreign invaders. It was superseded as the most important ceremonial center by La Venta, but this too was destroyed around 400 BCE, with some of its monumental artworks deliberately vandalized. One theory about the fall of the Olmecs suggests that flooding, due to a change in the course of local rivers, led people to abandon their settlements in the lowland Gulf Coast region. Another theory proposes that the

Maya began to dominate the Olmecs, taking over their trade routes and assimilating Olmec people into their own civilization. The same hot and humid climate that helped the Olmecs to become a successful agriculture-based society has also prevented archaeologists from finding out more about the Olmecs and the reason for their decline. This humidity has destroyed organic matter such as wood and cloth, so that in many sites all that remains of the civilization are its monumental sculptures.

Animal deities

The sculptures, together with smaller artworks and artifacts such as pottery and ax heads, reveal much about Olmec theology. It appears that their religion was pantheistic—it involved the worship of a large number of deities—and that many of their gods were either animals or part animal, part human. No named pantheon exists today, but the rich wildlife of the Gulf Coast of Mexico inspired belief in the divine powers of a wide range of creatures, including alligators, fish, jaguars, and snakes.

Many Olmec artworks depict supernatural creatures with a combination of human and animal features. In some cases, scholars believe that these artworks represented actual deities. In other cases they may well have been connected with Olmec rulers, who were either shamanic figures who used magic to change forms or who were believed to be directly descended from sacred animals. A monumental sculpture discovered at La Venta depicts a seated figure, possibly a ruler, with jaguars shown on the side of the carving. The jaguars may have symbolized the mythical origins of Olmec rulers from these animals.

Further evidence that the Olmecs believed their kings had the power to transform themselves into animals comes from an inscribed basalt stone discovered at La Mojarra, northwest of San Lorenzo. The stone contains 21 columns of glyphs, which were used in a writing system. Translators

The Olmecs and the Ball Game

It is likely that the Olmecs were the first people in Mesoamerica to play the ball game, a ritualistic sport that seems to have had deadly consequences for some of its players. Although the rules have not survived, evidence from the Mayan sites of Chichén Itzá and Zapotec shows that scores were accumulated either by passing the ball into one end of the court or another, or by hitting the ball through stone rings using only the head, elbows, and knees. For the Maya, the ball game seems to have been a symbolic reenactment of the conflict between the twin deities Hun Hunahpu and Vucub Hunahpu and the two lords of Xibalba, Hun Cam and Vucub Cam. A frieze at the Chichén Itzá ball court depicts a defeated team captain with a severed head. It is not known whether the same fate awaited defeated Olmec players, or whether the sport had similar mythological origins. It may even have been the victors who were sacrificed. Although the details are scant, it is known that the Olmecs played this game before the Maya. Rubber balls have been discovered at Olmec sites such as La Venta and San Lorenzo. According to one theory, the helmets shown in some Olmec images are the players' protective headgear.

Below: The ball court at Zapotec in the Oaxaca Valley, Mexico. The shape of the playing area resembles a capital letter I.

Key Olmec Sites

TLATILCO

EL VIEJÓN

GULF OF MEXICO

N

LAS BOCAS

CHALCATZINGO

CUELLO

TRES ZAPOTES

LA VENTA

BALANCÁN

TUXTLA MOUNTAINS

SAN LORENZO

CHIAPA DE CORZO

LAGUNA DE LOS CERROS

COPÁN

PACIFIC OCEAN

IZAPA

| 0 | 250 miles |
| 0 | 400 km |

found that it recorded the accomplishments of a king named Harvest Moon Lord who had the ability to transform himself into an animal. Dates inscribed on the stone correspond to 143 CE and 156 CE, several centuries after the decline of the Olmecs. However, the glyphs, in the Zoquean language, are thought to be a form of the ancestral Olmec linguistic system. The information about Harvest Moon Lord is echoed in earlier sculptures that show humanlike figures in various stages of transformation into jaguars. Examples of these sculptures include a kneeling human with the ears, muzzle, and mouth of a jaguar, and a long-tailed creature, generally jaguarlike but standing on its hind legs and with human fingers.

Examining the jaguar cult

Scholars believe that jaguar worship was a central part of Olmec religion, citing as evidence the number of images of half-human, half-jaguar figures at Olmec sites. One idea to explain the preponderance of such images is that, in Olmec mythology, a jaguar mated with a human, and from this union all Olmec kings were descended. In the jungles of southern Mexico the jaguar would have been one of the most impressive of all animals, flourishing on land, in water, and in trees. It is likely that these attributes gave the jaguar a supernatural status and led to its connection with shamans, who, it was believed, could pass from the spiritual world to the natural world and back again. Jaguar cults were prominent in many other Mesoamerican civilizations: one of the Mayan gods was known as Jaguar Baby, while

the Teotihuacános (people of a city-state northeast of Mexico City that was powerful in the first millennium CE) had a Temple of the Jaguars, which depicted the creature on its walls. The Aztecs, the last great Mesoamerican civilization before the Spanish conquest of 1521, had a military order known as the Jaguar Knights.

The Mother Culture of Mesoamerica?

In 1862 plantation workers in Huaypan, Veracruz, discovered a huge stone head buried in the ground. At first scholars thought the sculpture was the work of the Maya, who at the time were regarded as the earliest and most influential of all Mesoamerican civilizations. It was not until 1939, after the discovery of many more artworks and artifacts, that scholars finally agreed that these were archaeological relics of a civilization that predated the Maya, which they named Olmec for the peoples who inhabited the Gulf Coast region.

Many commentators have since described the Olmecs as the "mother culture" of Mesoamerica, citing its monumental architecture, language system, notion of kingship and rituals to support it, use of maize as a staple crop, trade networks, and sacred 260-day calendar as features that were taken up by the Mayan, Toltec, and Aztec civilizations, among others. Others believe, instead, that the Maya and the Olmecs were "sister cultures" who habitually borrowed beliefs and practices from each other.

Not everyone believes that the jaguar was the preeminent Olmec animal deity. Another theory is that many carvings that seem to be of jaguars are of serpents. This hypothesis is based on the observation that some carvings of so-called jaguar images have no teeth, while others have helmetlike headgear that represents scales. Moreover, while jaguar worship was common among hunting peoples, the Olmecs were mainly farmers who would more naturally have worshiped a creature associated with the earth, such as the serpent. Additional arguments in support of a serpent cult are that shoots of young corn plants resemble a snake's forked tongue and that kernels on a corncob look like a snake's scales. This theory, which further suggests that pyramids at sites such as La Venta represented the head of a huge Earth Serpent, remains controversial. What seems clear, however, is that Olmec belief in creatures that combined the characteristics of different animals influenced subsequent civilizations. In addition to half-human, half-animal figures, Olmec artists combined the feathers and claws of an eagle with the body of a serpent. Quetzalcoatl, a deity who took exactly this form, became one of the most significant Mesoamerican gods. The Teotihuacános worshiped him as a vegetation god; for the Toltecs (a Mesoamerican people who flourished between the 10th and 12th centuries CE), he was god of the morning and evening star; to the Aztecs, he symbolized death and rebirth.

Right: This Olmec bas-relief shows a priest making an offering to a snake deity.

Rituals and kingship

Religion and ritual reinforced the power of the elite in Olmec society. Agricultural and hunting lands were originally owned communally by kin groups; over time these lands came under the control of certain families who became the elite. One way in which the elite expressed its leadership was the construction of ceremonial centers, such as at San Lorenzo and La Venta, as well as Chalcatzingo, Laguna de los Cerros, and Tres Zapotes. The pyramids and plazas there were re-creations of the sacred landscape created by gods at the beginning of the world: pyramids represented mountains or volcanoes, stone columns were forests, and temple openings were caves. Just as images of humans changing into animals suggested kings' links to animal deities, so the elite's sacred buildings connected them with the gods of creation.

Throughout Mesoamerican history, human sacrifice and bloodletting enhanced rulers' power. While there is no firm evidence of human sacrifice among the Olmecs, there is evidence of bloodletting. Objects used in bloodletting rituals, including sharks' teeth, stingray spines, and obsidian blades, have been discovered at several Olmec sites. In addition, symbols on Olmec artworks and artifacts suggest that a fish deity was connected with the ritual of bloodletting. This fish deity also appears in Maya bloodletting imagery: in both cultures the practice of drawing blood was linked to the idea that rulers were descended from supernatural ancestors. The Maya seem to have developed the concept of bloodletting beyond the Olmec practice by making it essential to the process of legitimizing rulers and the survival of the natural world. However, it is likely that in this ritual, as in many others, the Olmecs were the innovators, and that their influence shaped the religions of many subsequent civilizations.

ANDREW CAMPBELL

Bibliography

Coe, Michael, and Rex Koontz. *Mexico: From the Olmecs to the Aztecs.* New York: Thames and Hudson, 2002.

Luckert, Karl W. *Olmec Religion: A Key to Middle America and Beyond.* Norman, OK: University of Oklahoma Press, 1976.

Scarre, Christopher, and Brian M. Fagan. *Ancient Civilizations.* New York: Longman, 1997.

SEE ALSO: Animals; Animal Worship; Aztecs; Blood; Maya; Quetzalcoatl; Sacrifice.

ORESTES

In Greek mythology Orestes is usually described as the son of Agamemnon and Clytemnestra, mythical king and queen of the ancient city of Mycenae, although in some accounts they are said to have come from nearby Argos, in Laconia. Orestes' life was blighted by the curse that his great-grandfather Pelops had brought on himself and all succeeding generations of his family.

The roots of the tragedy of Orestes can be traced back two generations before he was born. Pelops, founder of the Pelopid dynasty of Mycenae, wanted to marry Hippodameia. Hippodameia's father, Oenomaus, king of Pisa in Elis, would allow the union only if Pelops could beat him in a chariot race. Pelops won the contest by driving winged horses given to him by the sea god Poseidon and by offering a bribe to Myrtilus, Oenomaus's charioteer, to remove pins from his master's chariot. Oenomaus was killed, but Pelops drowned Myrtilus to avoid paying the bribe. As he was dying, Myrtilus cursed Pelops and his descendants. The numerous misfortunes that subsequently befell the house of Atreus, Pelops's son, are all attributed to this curse. Agamemnon was Atreus's son, and Orestes the son of Agamemnon.

The sins of the fathers

When Orestes was a baby, his father Agamemnon left home to lead the Greek armies in the Trojan War, leaving his wife, Clytemnestra, in charge of Mycenae. The campaign took a long time to prepare, and the war itself lasted 10 years, so Orestes was in his early teens by the time his father returned.

The Trojan War had not even begun when Agamemnon provoked the anger of the gods. While the Greeks were still gathering their fleet at the port of Aulis in readiness to transport their army to Troy, Agamemnon boasted that he was a better hunter than the goddess Artemis. To punish Agamemnon's hubris (pride), Artemis angrily stilled the winds so that the Greek ships could not set sail. A soothsayer told Agamemnon that the winds would return only if he sacrificed his daughter Iphigeneia to the offended goddess. With great sadness and reluctance, Agamemnon did his penance and had Iphigeneia killed on Artemis's altar. Clytemnestra never forgave her husband for allowing their daughter to be sacrificed and sought ways to avenge her death. Before long she joined forces with her cousin, Aegisthus, who hated Agamemnon as a consequence of an earlier conflict between their fathers, Thyestes and Atreus, respectively.

Left: Orestes consulting the oracle at Delphi. This marble bas-relief from the first century BCE was excavated from Herculaneum, one of the towns destroyed by an eruption of Mount Vesuvius in 79 CE.

Clytemnestra was at first reluctant to conspire with Aegisthus, but they later became lovers and she yielded to her desire for revenge and power. With Agamemnon away at Troy, the pair began to rule Mycenae as king and queen and made plans to kill Agamemnon when he returned. They forced Clytemnestra's surviving daughters to accept the new regime, but one of them, Electra, sent Orestes for safety to Agamemnon's ally Strophius, king of Phocis. That saved Orestes, for Aegisthus would not have allowed the heir to the throne to live.

When Agamemnon returned home to Mycenae with a mistress, the Trojan princess Cassandra, Clytemnestra and Aegisthus murdered the pair of them. They then ruled Mycenae for seven years. Orestes remained with Strophius, whose son Pylades became his close friend. When they reached manhood, they resolved to reclaim Orestes' birthright and avenge Agamemnon's death. They consulted the oracle of Apollo at Delphi, and Orestes was told to slay the killers of his father. The friends then proceeded to Mycenae and entered the city in secret. They made contact with Electra, who in one version had been compelled to marry a farmer so that her children would be ineligible to inherit the kingdom. Electra idolized her dead father and hated her mother and stepfather. She was therefore willing to help her brother. Together, the three young people managed to kill Aegisthus and Clytemnestra.

Although Orestes had acted with Apollo's approval, he was still guilty of matricide (killing one's mother), so he was vulnerable to attack by the Erinyes (Furies), goddesses of vengeance who tormented all criminals. These hideous demons pursued Orestes across Greece until he at last came to Athens. There a group of citizens assembled to hear his case, which Apollo defended since he originally supported Orestes' cause. The prosecution was presented according to some accounts by the Erinyes, in others by Clytemnestra's father, Tyndareos, or by Erigone, daughter of Aegisthus and Clytemnestra. The jury was divided, so Athena, the city's patron goddess, cast the deciding vote. Since Athena herself was born directly from Zeus and had no mother, she sympathized with Agamemnon as a father

figure. She ruled that Orestes' revenge was justifiable homicide. After she delivered her verdict the Erinyes agreed to become patrons of Athens, and were renamed the Eumenides ("Kindly Ones").

In search of a cure for madness

Despite his acquittal, Orestes' mind was still disturbed by all that had happened, so he and Pylades went in search of a cure for his madness. On the instructions of an oracle, they went to retrieve a sacred wooden image of Artemis from the Taurians, a savage northern people who were known to kill strangers on sight. Orestes and Pylades secretly entered the temple where the image

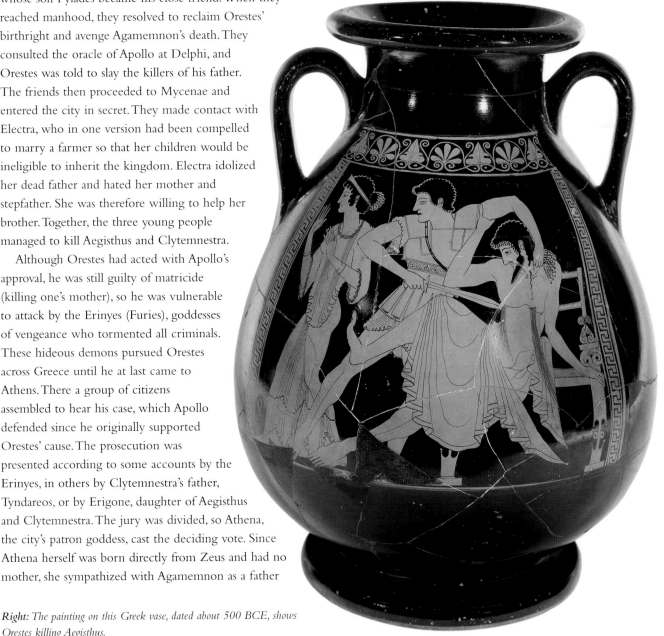

Right: The painting on this Greek vase, dated about 500 BCE, shows Orestes killing Aegisthus.

The Many Oresteias

The story of Orestes, otherwise known as the Oresteia, is represented in virtually every period of ancient Greek literature and art. An early and influential account of the Oresteia is elaborated in the *Odyssey*, an epic poem attributed to Homer (c. ninth–eighth century BCE). The poem refers to the seduction of Clytemnestra by Aegisthus, implicates both in the death of Agamemnon, and praises Orestes for killing Aegisthus. The Erinyes, Electra, and Pylades do not appear in Homer, and neither do the killing of Clytemnestra nor Orestes' trial. *Catalogues of Women*, a fragmentary epic attributed to Hesiod (fl. c. 800 BCE), mentions the sacrifice of Iphigeneia, the affair between Aegisthus and Clytemnestra, and her murder by Orestes.

A number of lyric poets who were familiar with the work of Homer and Hesiod also refer to the Oresteia. Stesichorus (fl. 600–550 BCE) wrote a long poem on the subject that includes a recognition scene between Electra and Orestes, and his pursuit by the Erinyes. Supporting characters emerge in an ode by Pindar (c. 522–c. 438 BCE) in which Orestes is saved from Aegisthus by a nurse named Arsinoe and taken in by King Strophius. These poems emphasize Clytemnestra's role in Agamemnon's death, and Orestes' role in hers, while the Homeric account plays down these events. Stesichorus and Pindar both locate Agamemnon's kingdom in Amyclae, a town near Sparta, not Mycenae.

The Oresteia is best known, however, from plays by the major tragedians of fifth-century-BCE Athens—Aeschylus (525–456 BCE), Sophocles (c. 496–406 BCE), and Euripides (c. 486–c. 406 BCE). Each develops the storyline in his own way, often by focusing on the female characters. All three set the action in Argos.

The *Oresteia* of Aeschylus is a trilogy consisting of *Agamemnon*, *Choephoroe* (*Libation Bearers*), and *Eumenides*. The three plays focus on the duty of children to their fathers and justify the role of the state in settling family feuds. Aeschylus's Clytemnestra manipulates her weak husband and justifies killing him with powerful rhetoric; Aegisthus is comparatively feeble, appearing only after the killing. As in the *Odyssey*, Orestes' deeds are praiseworthy, but Aeschylus confronts conflicting loyalties that the epic ignores. Electra plays a small role in Aeschylus's trilogy, and Pylades appears only to steel his friend's resolve to carry through the matricide. Aeschylus develops both the role of the Furies and the trial of Orestes more than any of his predecessors.

Sophocles may have been present at the first performance of Aeschylus's *Oresteia* in 458 BCE. In his own surviving play on this theme, *Electra*, the heroine is a passionate young woman and the driving force behind the plot to avenge her father, Agamemnon. Orestes is fairly passive, relying on Electra and a servant to direct his actions; Pylades is a silent character. Sophocles' Clytemnestra and Aegisthus are wicked and tyrannical; Orestes does not hesitate to kill his mother, and no Furies appear.

At about the same time as Sophocles was writing, Euripides was creating a unique vision of the Oresteia in four plays of his own: *Electra*, *Iphigeneia in Tauris*, *Orestes*, and *Iphigeneia at Aulis*. Euripides depicts Orestes and Pylades as homicidal thugs, while Clytemnestra is sympathetic and Aegisthus a popular leader. It was Euripides who first made Electra a farmer's wife, and he who developed the reunion of Orestes and Iphigeneia. Electra and Orestes regret the killings; the Erinyes are his guilty conscience.

Below: The story of Orestes appears on the side of the Sarcophagus of the Poet, a tomb from the third century BCE.

Above: After their murder of Aegisthus and Clytemnestra, Orestes, Electra, and Pylades are pursued by the Furies (Erinyes). This engraving originally appeared in an 18th-century dictionary of mythology.

was kept, but they were discovered and sent by the Taurian king Thoas to be sacrificed by the priestess of Artemis. The priestess, however, turned out to be Iphigeneia. She had not after all died at Aulis, but had been spirited away to serve Artemis in Tauris. Iphigeneia helped her brother, and she, Orestes, and Pylades escaped together. They fled with the sacred image—in some versions of the story, they took it to Athens, in others to the island of Rhodes.

Pylades then married Electra, and they seem to have lived happily ever after. Orestes, however, was less fortunate. In one version of events, he was due to wed his cousin Hermione, daughter of Agamemnon's brother Menelaus, but during one of his fits of madness she was carried off by Pyrrhus (also known as Neoptolemus), a distinguished Trojan war veteran. Orestes pursued them and killed Pyrrhus in Apollo's temple at Delphi.

Torment to the end

Most accounts agree, however, that Orestes finally did marry Hermione, and had a son, Tisamenus, who later ruled Achaea. However, Orestes did not remain with his family for long. As an additional reparation for killing his mother, or perhaps as a penance for killing Pyrrhus on ground that was sacred to Apollo, he had to endure a year's exile in Arcadia, a region of the Peloponnese peninsula in southern Greece. There he was bitten by a snake and died. He was buried near the city of Tegea.

The curse upon the house of Atreus was so strong that, even in death, Orestes did not find a permanent resting place. A Spartan, acting on instructions from an oracle, later dug up his bones and brought them to Sparta. The Spartans believed that once they were in possession of these relics, they would vanquish their neighbors and perpetual enemies the Tegeans. This seems to have been no more than wishful thinking, for in reality the Tegeans continued to be formidable opponents in battle, and it was diplomacy, rather than war, that finally brought them into the great Hellenic military alliance known as the League of Sparta.

JIM MARKS

Bibliography

Aeschylus, and Robert Fagles, trans. *The Oresteia*. New York: Penguin USA, 1984.

Homer, and Robert Fagles, trans. *The Odyssey*. New York: Penguin USA, 1999.

SEE ALSO: Agamemnon; Artemis; Athena; Atreus; Clytemnestra; Furies; Iphigeneia; Pelops.

ORION

In ancient Greek mythology, Orion was a giant hunter. He features in numerous legends, many of which give contradictory accounts of his life and exploits. Every version agrees, however, that after his death he became a constellation in the night sky—the outline of the group of stars named for him appears to show the hunter wearing a lion's skin, carrying a club, and accompanied by two hunting dogs.

Below: One of the brightest star clusters in the night sky, the constellation named for Orion has inspired artists for thousands of years.

In most accounts, Orion was either the son of Hyreius, king of Boeotia, or of the deities Dionysus and Demeter. A few myths state that his mother was Gaia, the earth goddess; elsewhere his parents are said to have been either Poseidon and Euryale or Hyrieus and the nymph Clonia. One myth attributed Orion's origin to a bull hide: childless Hyrieus asked for an heir by sacrificing a bull to Zeus, Hermes, and Poseidon; they urinated on the hide, and Orion was born from it.

Love stories

As a young man Orion courted Merope, one of the Pleiades, seven nymphs who were companions of the Greek goddess Artemis (the others were Alcyone, Celaeno, Electra, Maia, Sterope, and Taygete). Merope rejected his advances. In one story, she married a mortal, Sisyphus, king of Corinth. According to another version, Merope became betrothed to Orion, but her father—Oenopion, king of Chios, an island in the Aegean Sea—kept postponing the

date of the wedding. Eventually Orion lost patience and raped Merope; Oenopion blinded him in revenge. Orion then wandered helplessly until the god Hephaestus took pity on him and sent his own attendant, Kedalion, to help the blinded man. Sitting on top of Orion's shoulders, Kedalion guided him to the abode of Helios, the sun god, and Eos, goddess of the dawn. When Eos saw Orion she was moved to tears—they became the glistening morning dew—and immediately restored his sight. On seeing his savior, Orion fell in love with her, but this angered the gods, who ordered Artemis, goddess of hunting, to slay the man with her arrows. Before he died, however, Orion repaid his debt to Hephaestus by building a subterranean temple in his honor in Sicily. He also built walls around the island's coast to protect it from the sea.

Another legend states that Orion and Artemis fell in love and planned to marry. Their relationship was sabotaged by Artemis's brother, Apollo, who disapproved of the union between a goddess and a human. Apollo pointed to a small bobbing object far out to sea and challenged Artemis to hit it. The goddess would never turn down a chance to show off her marksmanship, so she shot an arrow from her bow and hit the center of the distant speck. The target disappeared beneath the waves. Not long afterward the body of the victim was washed up on shore—it was

Above: This 19th-century engraving shows Orion, on a hunting expedition, being fatally bitten by a scorpion.

Orion, as Apollo well knew. Artemis, grief-stricken, asked Zeus to place her dead lover among the stars.

Several mythological accounts of the life of Orion end with his being stung fatally by a scorpion. According to some sources, the venomous creature was set upon him by Artemis after he had raped one of her followers. In other accounts, Orion boasted that he could slay any animal, so the scorpion was his comeuppance. In a variation on this theme, the earth goddess Gaia sent the scorpion. It stung Orion, but he survived thanks to an antidote promptly administered by Asclepius, god of medicine.

A modern place among the stars

Every legend of Orion agrees that after the hunter's death, Zeus granted the wish of Artemis and placed him in the heavens. The constellation still known as Orion, the Hunter, is the most spectacular and one of the most easily recognized in the sky. The stars represent the hunter holding a shield in his left hand and a club in his right. Betelgeuse, one of the largest stars known, marks his right shoulder. Bellatrix marks his left shoulder, and Saiph and Rigel mark his two legs. Other notable parts of the

The Australian Pleiades

The Aboriginal peoples of Australia have their own myth of the creation of the Pleiades and Orion, which are visible in the southern hemisphere during Australia's winter months. The Pleiades were seven beautiful sisters who roamed the land during the day and returned to their sky home at night. A man named Wurrunnah captured two of them but discovered that their beautiful hair was like icicles. He tried to melt the sisters' cold crystals over his campfire; the water put out his fire and dimmed the sisters' brightness (thus accounting for the two dimmest stars of the Pleiades). During their captivity, many men admired the sisters, but Berai Berai (two brothers) honored them most. They hunted for food for the sisters but knew that they longed for their home in the sky. Each night, their five sisters twinkled, beckoning them. One day Wurrunnah told the sisters to gather pine bark from a tree. As they began, the pine tree extended itself to the sky, and the sisters escaped home. Berai Berai laid aside their weapons and mourned until death's shadow overtook them. The fairies then placed Berai Berai in the sky, where they could always hear the sisters singing; the brothers became Orion's sword and belt.

Other Myths about Orion's Belt

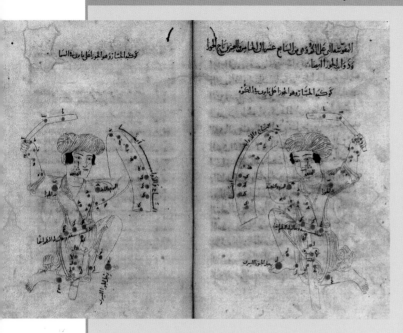

Above: The constellation of Orion appears in the Book of Fixed Stars, *an Arabic astronomical treatise of the 11th century CE.*

Many peoples saw significance in the three bright stars of Orion's belt—which today we call Mintaka, Alnilam, and Alnitak—that form an almost straight line. Peruvians believed the middle star was a criminal; the moon goddess sent Pata, the two outside stars, to capture him. In South African myth, Orion associated with Isilimela (the Pleiades), daughters of a sky god. Their husband (the star Aldebaran) unsuccessfully shot an arrow (Orion's sword) at three zebras (Orion's belt), and remained in the cold sky: he dared not return without game, and he dared not retrieve his arrow; a fierce lion (Betelgeuse) watched the zebras. In other South African myths, Orion's belt stars were lions that had been transformed by a magical girl child, and three pigs chased by three dogs. Siberians and Mongolians saw stags, while California Native Americans saw mountain sheep, antelope, and deer. Hindu myth said the belt stars were an arrow fired at creator-god Prajapati, who lusted after his daughter (Aldebaran). Northern Australian Aboriginals saw three fishers in a canoe, as did the Wasco of Oregon. Ancient Jews saw Nimrod, bound to the heavens for disobeying God. Early French agriculturalists called Orion's belt *le râteau* (the rake).

constellation include Orion's belt, consisting of three bright stars and including the dark Horsehead nebula; and Orion's sword, where the bright Orion nebula is visible to the naked eye. The constellation is located near the celestial equator and dominates the night sky of the northern hemisphere in winter. The nearby constellations of Canis Major and Canis Minor represent Orion's two hunting dogs. Also in the same part of the sky is Taurus, the Bull, which was often seen as Orion's prey. Among the stars of this constellation are the Pleiades—this is particularly an allusion to Orion's pursuit of Merope, but also to a version of the story in which Orion pursues the seven sisters and their mother, Pleione, until the gods turn them into doves.

Another astronomical reference to the story of Orion is the constellation of Scorpius, the Scorpion, which is never visible at the same time as Orion—according to legend, that is because Zeus ordered the killer and its victim to be kept apart.

Similar legends in other cultures

The legends of Orion and his link with the stars have notable parallels in other ancient cultures. Sumerians saw the constellation as Sibzianna, a shepherd god; the neighboring stars were his flock. Mesopotamians called it

Uru-anna (Light of Heaven), who, as Gilgamesh, battled Gut-anna (Bull of Heaven), which is represented by the Taurus constellation. What modern Westerners know as Orion was known to Hittites as Aqhat, a hunter. The battle goddess Anat loved Aqhat, but Aqhat rejected her and refused to lend her his bow. Anat sent a man to steal it, but the man killed Aqhat. Aqhat fell into the sea, an explanation for the constellation's disappearance below the horizon in spring. The ancient Egyptians were among the many other civilizations that attached mythic significance to the constellation. They regarded it as a manifestation of Osiris in his sky barge.

ALYS CAVINESS

Bibliography

Bulfinch, Thomas. *Bulfinch's Mythology.* New York: Modern Library, 1998.

Gayley, Charles Mills. *The Classic Myths in English Literature and Art.* Boston: Ginn and Company, 1893.

Hamilton, Edith. *Mythology.* Boston: Little, Brown and Company, 1942.

Ovid, and A. D. Melville, trans. *Metamorphoses.* New York: Oxford University Press, 1998.

SEE ALSO: Apollo; Artemis; Asclepius; Australia; Demeter; Dionysus; Eos; Gaia; Hephaestus; Osiris; Pleiades; Poseidon; Zeus.

ORPHEUS

In Greek mythology, Orpheus was a musician from Thrace, a region occupying parts of what are now eastern Greece and western Turkey. There are many legends about his magical skill on the lyre, which enabled him to charm trees, rivers, and stones, as well as wild beasts.

Below: This marble statue of Orpheus with his lyre was carved by French artist Pierre de Francheville (1554–1618).

O rpheus was the son of Calliope, the Muse of epic poetry; in most versions of his story, his father was Oeagrus, a Thracian river god, one of the children of Ares. As a child Orpheus learned music from Apollo, the greatest master of the art. In some versions, Apollo is said to have been Orpheus's real father. Orpheus was a gifted pupil, and before long he was able to calm the people of his native Thrace, who were notorious for their barbarism, by playing to them on his lyre, a stringed instrument, which he had had fashioned out of a hollow tortoise shell. According to one legend, Orpheus invented the cithara, a stringed musical instrument that was widely used in ancient Greece. Similar in shape to the lyre, it had from 5 to 11 strings that were plucked with a plectrum or with the fingers. The guitar and the zither derive their names from the cithara.

Adventures with the Argonauts

Orpheus had many adventures. For example, he accompanied Jason and the Argonauts on their voyage to retrieve the Golden Fleece. While they were at sea, he calmed the waves during storms, distracted the Sirens who were trying to ensnare the crew with their songs, and quietened the sailors when they became unruly. According to some accounts, it was Orpheus who lulled the dragon to sleep so that Jason could grab the Golden Fleece.

On his return to Thrace, Orpheus lived in a cave and spent his time charming the countryside with his music. He fell passionately in love with the Dryad Eurydice and wanted to marry her. On their wedding day, however, many dreadful things happened. Hymen, god of marriage, came to the ceremony. This was normally an auspicious sign of a good life ahead for the happy couple, but on this occasion Hymen was unable to keep his sacred wedding torch alight. No matter how much he shook it or blew on it, it just produced smoke that irritated the eyes of the guests and made them cry. That was a bad omen. The same day, Eurydice was chased through the meadows by Aristaeus, the son of Apollo and Cyrene and the husband of Autonoe. He was herdsman and beekeeper to the gods. As Eurydice fled from him, his bees pursued her; she accidentally stepped on a snake, which bit her. She died as a result.

Orpheus in the underworld

Orpheus was overwhelmed with grief by the death of Eurydice. He ceased to sing and play and instead moped around in silence. Finally he resolved to search for the entrance to the underworld so that he could at least see—and, if possible, retrieve—his lost love. When he found the entrance in southern Italy, he made his way into the passage. Once inside, he began to play his lyre again. The

Below: A mosaic from the third century CE from Tarsus, Turkey, shows Orpheus playing his lyre and enchanting animals and charming birds from the trees.

Enduring Myth

The story of Orpheus is one of the oldest Greek myths. Its enduring popularity has given rise to many variations on the basic legend, as each new teller has added his or her own embellishments. In particular, the imagery of the story of this musical hero, master of the lyre and inventor of the cithara, was adopted by the esoteric religious movement known as Orphism to reinforce and legitimize its doctrine. It has also been invoked by many poets for inspiration. As an allegory, the pagan story even found its way into early Christian iconography. In the catacombs of Jerusalem, for example, Jesus was depicted in the guise of Orpheus with the lyre. In some later Christian tombs Orpheus is shown delivering the Sermon on the Mount or acting as "the Good Shepherd."

One of the myth's most potent and enduring images is of the power of music to achieve effects that are unattainable by other means. Orpheus used his celestial harmonies in an attempt to raise Eurydice from the dead and influence the shades of the underworld. If he had not made the mistake of looking back, he would probably have succeeded—the technique was faultless, only the practitioner was flawed by his humanity. Such ideas are more than artistic fantasy. A modern form of psychological treatment known as music therapy uses harmonious sounds to calm anguished people and improve their state of mind.

music that he played charmed Charon, the boatman of the Styx River, and Cerberus, the three-headed dog that guarded the entrance to Hades, into letting him pass. All the inhabitants of the underworld were likewise captivated by Orpheus's music: even Tartarus stopped torturing the souls of his victims. In *Metamorphoses*, Roman poet Ovid (43 BCE–17 CE) described the scene this way: "Tantalus stopped reaching for the receding waters, the wheel of Ixion stopped in wonder, the vultures ceased tearing at the liver of Tityus, the Danaid sisters left their urns empty, and Sisyphus sat on his throne to listen." In the *Georgics*, Virgil (70–19 BCE) described how thousands of flitting shades and spectral images of the departed flocked to see Orpheus, moved by his music. The Furies abandoned their vengeful ways to listen to his song. Death itself seemed suspended.

Even the gods Hades and Persephone were softened and were temporarily rendered speechless by the sound of Orpheus's lyre. The grieving hero took this opportunity to explain to them how his bride Eurydice had died before her time. He implored them to let her return with him to earth, pointing out that they would inevitably have her back in their kingdom one day, so a temporary reprieve

Above: This oil painting by the German artist Friedrich Brentel (1580–1651) depicts the ascent of Orpheus from the underworld. Eurydice is dragged back into Hades when Orpheus turns to look at her.

would make no difference. Desperately, Orpheus then announced that he would not, and could not, return without her. Moved by his appeals and the intensity of his devotion, the gods decided to let Orpheus take Eurydice, but on one condition: he must lead the way out of the underworld and not look back at her until they reached the upper air. Orpheus agreed. So he departed, his beloved behind him, his eyes fixed ahead.

While he was leading her up the steep path through the black vapors, however, just as the end of the passage was in sight and light was visible ahead, he could not refrain from turning and gazing at his wife's face—he wanted to make sure that she was still with him. At that very moment, Eurydice turned into a mist. Orpheus tried to grab her but could not prevent her from being sucked back into the underworld. Hermes, the escort of souls, led her down the path into the dark abode. Orpheus tried to follow, but this time even his music failed to overcome the guards. Charon would not allow him back on the boat.

Above: Orpheus leads Eurydice out of the underworld. This painting is one of the greatest works by the French painter Jean-Baptiste-Camille Corot (1796–1875).

Orpheus reluctantly returned to the world above and became like a lost soul on earth, wandering here and there, living as a recluse, avoiding the company, above all, of women. He still sang, but only songs of mourning and lament. He remained attractive to women, however, and many of them tried to cajole him out of his devotion to his dead lover. Yet Orpheus remained adamant that he would have nothing to do with any other female.

Death of a hero
One day on his aimless wanderings Orpheus happened upon a group of Thracian women who were taking part in an orgiastic ritual in honor of Dionysus, god of wine and intoxication. When they saw Orpheus, they went into a frenzy and rushed after him. Their weapons, however, fell to the ground around him, charmed by his music. The women grew more hostile and bold, abandoning all restraint. As they began to play their raucous Dionysian music, the curved pipes, pounding drums, and whooping and shrieking all combined in a great cacophony that eventually drowned out the sound of the hero's lyre.

The women were able to capture Orpheus. They ripped him to shreds with their bare hands. Their crime is usually said to have been motivated by their anger at having had their amatory advances rejected—as English playwright William Congreve (1670–1729) put it, "Hell hath no fury like a woman scorned." Some accounts, however, claim that their actions were inspired by Dionysus himself, who resented Orpheus's advocacy of the worship of Apollo.

As the women tore him apart, Orpheus's head rolled down a hill into the Hebrus River and was washed down to the sea, rolling this way and that and constantly crying, "Eurydice! Eurydice!" Eventually it came ashore on the island of Lesbos. The local inhabitants placed the talking head in a cave, where it functioned as an oracle for those who came with questions. Orpheus was said to have inspired the work of Sappho (fl. c. 610–580 BCE), a great female poet who lived on Lesbos. In another legend, Orpheus was torn apart by Maenads—the Muses gathered the pieces of his dismembered corpse and buried them in a single place near their home on Mount Olympus. A nightingale sang over the tomb of Orpheus, and his musical instrument was placed in the heavens as a constellation. This is the modern Lyra, the brightest star of which is Vega.

The cult of Orphism

The cave on Lesbos containing the head of Orpheus functioned for many years as an oracle until one day the head ceased to speak. Much of what it had said had been recorded, however, and this information formed the basis of a new religion that emerged around 600 BCE. Orphism, as it was known, claimed to have at its core the revelations given by the head of Orpheus after it had been detached from his body. The records—known as the Orphica—contain hymns, poetry, and commentaries.

Orphism developed an elaborate cosmogony (a theory explaining the creation of the universe) that focused on the killing and eating of Dionysus by the Titans and Zeus's subsequent destruction of the Titans, from whose ashes arose the human race, part Dionysiac (divine and good) and part Titan (earthly and evil). Through initiation into the Orphic mysteries, and by living an ascetic life of abstention from meat, wine, and sexual activity, individuals sought to suppress their earthly nature. Full liberation of the divine soul could be achieved only through a cycle of incarnations. Orphism was never a widespread cult, although its ideas were influential.

Thus, in Greek mythology, Orpheus evolved from a gifted musician into a theologian of unassailable authority. The explanation of this development is to be found in the myth itself. Orpheus had achieved something that few mortals had ever done: he had entered Hades as a living being and reemerged from it unscathed. In essence, he had conquered death and thereby weakened its fearful grip on humankind. In addition, Orpheus's round-trip to the underworld cast reassuring new light on the mystery of death by opening up the possibility of rebirth. Orphian scholars concluded that their hero had been forbidden to turn around and look at Eurydice while they were emerging from the underworld because by doing so he would have been able to see something the gods did not

Below: The story of Orpheus has remained perennially popular in art. In this French oil painting of the late 19th century, he is shown on the seashore lamenting the death of Eurydice on their wedding day.

Left: This painting by Gustave Moreau (1826–1898) shows Orpheus's detached head in the arms of a suitor after he had forsworn all contact with women.

Orphic Religion

Central to Orphic religious practices was the belief in the transmigration of souls, which, if properly understood and dealt with, could lead to ultimate bliss on the Isles of the Blessed or in the realm of the starry ether. The goal of every Orphic disciple was to learn how the human soul had become stained with evil and the means by which it could be purified. Orpheus had taught the proper rituals and incantations necessary for purification, and he recommended a lifestyle of asceticism that included vegetarianism, a general respect for the value of all life, expiation of sins, and sanctity of conduct. Orphics dressed in white to indicate their aspirations to purity, and they did everything in their power to avoid any form of impropriety. The strict rules of Orphism, together with the prominence it gave to music, caused the cult to be identified with other mystery religions, such as the Bacchanalia and the Eleusinian Mysteries of Demeter. The revelations witnessed by these cults tended to result in joy and the hope for an afterlife of bliss.

want him to see; namely, the process of regeneration. Thus the very act that stole Eurydice from Orpheus forever is the same act that revealed to him the secret that all humans would like to share.

Orphism in art

Since the decline of Orphism as a religious cult, the term has come to denote the style of painting created and practiced by French painter Robert Delaunay (1885–1941). First called "orphic cubism" by French poet Guillaume Apollinaire (1880–1918), the style is characterized by an approach in which color (identified with light) is the primary pictorial element. The theory on which orphic cubism is based comes from the recognition that the constant movements and changes of light produce color

shapes that are independent of objects, and that create patterns resembling those of abstraction. By an extension of this theory, certain combinations of colors can be juxtaposed in such a way as to produce harmonic contrasts with each other and thus represent the movement of light. Delaunay's series *The Windows*, painted between 1910 and 1913, exemplifies the kaleidoscopic possibilities of orphism, as does his *Window on the City No. 4* (1911). Orphism was built on the achievements of earlier movements such as impressionism, cubism, and futurism, and especially on the 19th-century color theories studied and explored by, among others, Georges Seurat (1859–1891), the French artist who founded pointillism. In modern English usage, the term *Orphian* or *Orphean* means anything that is outstandingly melodious or tuneful.

KIRK SUMMERS

Bibliography
Bulfinch, Thomas. *Myths of Greece and Rome.* New York: Viking Penguin, 1979.

Ovid, and A. D. Melville, trans. *Metamorphoses.* New York: Oxford University Press, 1998.

SEE ALSO: Apollo; Demeter; Dionysus; Hades; Jason; Maenads; Muses; Mystery Cults; Persephone.

OSIRIS

Osiris, god of the dead and the underworld, was one of the most important deities in ancient Egypt. A fertility god in the Predynastic Period (before c. 2925 BCE), he had by about 2400 BCE become also a funerary god and the personification of dead pharaohs. Legend has it that Osiris was buried at Abydos, a great necropolis in Egypt's Western Desert.

Osiris was one of four or five children of earth god Geb and sky goddess Nut. All accounts agree that Osiris had two sisters—Isis and Nepthys—and at least one brother, Seth, although occasionally Thoth, ibis-headed god of wisdom, is added as a second male sibling. Osiris was said to have been born in the Western Desert near Memphis. The four siblings were paired off with each other, Isis to Osiris, and Nepthys to Seth. Their marriages symbolized the organization of the universe: Isis and Osiris represented light, fertility, order, and life, while Seth and Nepthys symbolized—and were agents of—darkness, sterility, chaos, and death.

Below: The valley of the Nile near Luxor, Egypt. Osiris was the god of all the fertile land along the river.

As the firstborn son, Osiris inherited the best parts of Egypt. His kingdom—known as Kemet—was the band of fertile black soil along the banks of the Nile River, which was practically the only extensive tract of habitable land in the whole region. As a god, Osiris came to be seen as the personification of fertility: he is said to have introduced Egyptians to agriculture.

Seth, the younger son, had the desert as his territory. The deep desert, where no human could survive for long and whose unpredictable sandstorms were greatly feared, came to represent chaos in the Egyptian mind. The desert areas near the edges of cultivation were comparably inhospitable and frightening. Hyenas and jackals lived there, together with lions and wild bulls, which were hunted by Egyptian kings until the first millennium BCE. The desert was also home to Libyan and Bedouin groups who raided Egyptian outposts. The contrast between the wild, hostile, dangerous desert and the civilized, fertile land along the riverbank struck the Egyptians very strongly. The counterpoint was reflected in their stories of Osiris and Seth.

Fratricide

Seth was jealous of Osiris and plotted to kill him and take over his kingdom. After he murdered his brother, he hacked the body into pieces and scattered the pieces throughout Egypt. The exact number of pieces varies from version to version, but it is traditionally 14. Many cities claimed to have received pieces of the corpse: according to tradition, Osiris's head was buried in Abydos, his leg on the island of Biga. In some versions of the story, his phallus was buried at Memphis.

After the death of her brother-husband, the faithful Isis set out to reassemble his body. She was aided by Anubis, jackal-headed god of embalming, and Nepthys, who did not support her husband's action. After reconstructing Osiris's body, Isis was able to bring him to life for a short time, during which she conceived their son Horus. However, according to *maat*, the correct order of the universe (see box, opposite),

Osiris, although temporarily revived, could not remain on earth. He was given the job of king and judge of the souls of the dead in the underworld. There, Osiris had no power over living mortals or gods, so he could not help his own son in the ensuing struggle against Seth for the throne.

In another version of the story, Seth killed his brother by luring Osiris into a coffinlike box. In early accounts the murderer acted alone, but according to the version common in Greco-Roman times there was a conspiracy between 72 men and a queen of Nubia. Once Osiris was captured, they shut the lid of the box and cast it adrift. Eventually it washed up on the shores of the Mediterranean Sea near Byblos and became part of the trunk of a tree. This tree was later cut down and made into a column of a temple. Isis rescued the body in its coffin from the temple at Byblos, then magically conceived Horus. However, she neglected her husband's body to care for the infant. In the account of this story, written by Plutarch (c. 46–120 CE), it was only at this point that Seth came upon the body and hacked it to pieces. Osiris's phallus was thrown into the Nile River and eaten by fish. This may explain the observation made by Herodotus (c. 484–425 BCE) that Egyptian priests were forbidden to eat fish.

Authoritative sources

There are many references to the story of Osiris in the Pyramid Texts (about 2400 BCE); in a long hymn to Osiris on a stela now housed in the Louvre in Paris, France; in the New Kingdom story entitled "The Contendings of Horus and Seth;" and in various other funerary texts. However, no Egyptian account of the story of Osiris is complete. The most detailed version of the legend is found in Plutarch, but he was Greek and lived in the first and second centuries CE, by which time Osiris had largely been superseded.

Left: Dating from the Ptolemaic dynasty, this statuette of Osiris is made of bronze and varnished wood.

Osiris and the Concept of *Maat*

As well as symbolizing the cycle of nature, Osiris represented the forces of *maat*. This word is often translated as "truth," but it is a far more complex concept than that suggests. *Maat* also embraces the concept of rightness—in other words, that which should exist or the way things ought to be. "Cosmic order" is probably closer to the ancient Egyptians' understanding of the word.

When Osiris became ruler of Egypt, with Isis as his queen, he made Egypt a civilized country, establishing agriculture, law, and worship of the gods. The myth of Osiris symbolized the transmission of *maat* through the kingship. The king (pharaoh) was regarded as the embodiment of *maat*. While alive, he was Horus, the personification of the forces of *maat*. When he died, he became Osiris, a ruler in the underworld and the arbiter of justice. As god of the underworld, he sat enthroned. Dead people who had been properly buried came before him there to have their hearts weighed. If they were free of wrongdoing, their hearts would balance perfectly with the ostrich feather of *maat* that rested on the other side of the balance. The dead were then no longer dead but reborn and rejuvenated, and they could look forward to everlasting existence.

Although Herodotus lived during the height of Osiris's power, he, too, was Greek. The writer devoted almost a whole book to the customs of the Egyptians, describing many of their festivals and temples, including those of Osiris and Isis. His *History* is informative and readable, but it remains the work of an outsider who regarded Egyptian practices as rather strange. Diodorus Siculus (90–21 BCE), another Greek, wrote about Egyptian religion, although he focused primarily on the worship of Isis.

Osiris in the heavens

In addition to being god of the underworld, Osiris was also linked with the sky. He was sometimes described as "he who lives in Sahu, spending one season in the sky and one on earth." The ancient Egyptian Sahu was the constellation known in modern astronomy as Orion. Sahu was believed to represent the most recently deceased pharaoh, who was identified with Osiris. Each night Orion disappears below the horizon. To ancient inhabitants of the Nile Valley, this represented the dead king leaving the world of the living and entering the underworld. However, in the same way as the stars rose again each night, the dead pharaoh would be reborn.

Just as Isis knelt grieving at the foot of Osiris after his murder, the star Sopdet is located below Sahu in the sky. Sopdet, also called Sothis in late Egyptian history, is known today as Sirius (the Dog Star). Sirius is associated with the heat of summer, which is the time when the Nile River floods. The rising of Sopdet in conjunction with the sun reaching its zenith in the sky took place in mid-July in the modern calendar. The flood was essential

Right: This Egyptian stela, made of wood and stucco, depicts the deities (left to right) Horus, Nepthys, Isis, Osiris, and Anubis.

Images of Osiris

Unlike some other pharaonic deities of ancient Egypt, Osiris was nearly always shown as a human male. He is frequently depicted as a wrapped mummy with his hands emerging from the winding sheets to hold two scepters. On his head is a special crown, and a false beard hangs from his chin. The beard is braided and curled at the end, a style of facial hair reserved only for gods or for humans who have become divine. (The beard is known to be false because the straps holding it on are visible on the side of the face.)

Osiris's headgear is a combination of the white crown worn by pharaohs and two large ostrich feathers. The white crown is tall and shaped a little like a slender bulb. It is often worn by pharaohs (but never by Osiris) in combination with the red crown. On its own, the white crown is associated with Upper Egypt (the Valley), while the red crown represents Lower Egypt (the Delta). However, paintings of Osiris make it clear that his crown is not white. Instead it is shown in stripes of different colors, and it seems to be formed of papyrus plants. No one knows for sure what the crowns of ancient Egyptian kings and queens were made of. Golden circlets with cobras on the brow have been found, but none of the helmetlike headdresses—these survive only in pictures. Scholars have suggested that they may have been made of leather or wicker.

Left: This bronze statuette, sculpted between about 775 and 332 BCE, depicts Isis protecting her husband-brother Osiris.

to the lives of everyone in the Nile Valley, so the star and its associated goddesses became very important. In fact, Sopdet was an important deity from around 3400 BCE. Later she became identified with Isis, and her individual personality was lost in that of the more famous goddess. In the Pyramid Texts, the king, who was identified with Osiris, was said to marry his sister Sopdet. She then gave birth to the Morning Star (Venus). In the familiar myths, Isis married Osiris and gave birth to Horus. In their astral manifestations, however, they were Sahu and Sopdet, and their child was not Horus but Sopdu. One of the titles of Sopdu was "Lord of the East." This is usually taken to mean that Sopdu guarded the borders of Egypt. Sometimes he is symbolized by an ancient desert warrior in plumed headgear. Like the other personalities of Horus, Sopdu was represented as a falcon or hawk. Unlike them, however, Sopdu was seldom shown in part-human form. He was more often depicted as a crouching falcon wearing a

headdress made of falcon feathers and holding a scepter resembling the flail traditionally held by pharaohs.

Versatile deity

As one of the most enduring and important Egyptian deities, Osiris had many aspects. He was often known as Osiris Khenty-amentiu, "Osiris Foremost of Westerners." *Westerners* in this context are the dead, who were imagined to have "gone to rest" below the western horizon, like the sun. Osiris was also known as Osiris Wenen-Nefer, which more or less means "Osiris in a State of Perfection." Some scholars believe that Wenen-Nefer was originally the name of another god of death; others that the term refers to the fact that the mummified Osiris will not decay but will stay forever "perfect." His symbols included the Djed pillar, a column with four horizontal bars across the upper end and a sun disk or two falcon feathers on top.

During the Middle Kingdom (c. 1938–c. 1630 BCE), Egyptians dramatized the story of Osiris. Osirian rites took the form of enactments of scenes from the myth in a sort of passion play. The rituals also included great processions and sometimes the construction of a new shrine for the god. Such customs were mentioned more than a thousand years later by Herodotus, who likened them to a mystery cult such as that of Dionysus. He also described "a great festival of Isis in the city of Busiris," which celebrated the story of Osiris and Isis and at which animals were sacrificed and crowds of worshipers beat their breasts and mourned.

Serapis

On earth Osiris took the form of the sacred bull, Apis. From the combined name Osiris-Apis came Serapis. At first, Serapis was no more than another name for Osiris. Gradually, however, he came to be thought of as a separate god. By the time the last native ruler of Egypt was overthrown in 343 BCE, Serapis had begun to replace the original deity on whom he was based. During the reign of the Ptolemaic kings (304–30 BCE), he took over from Osiris as the consort of Isis and as deity of the afterlife. Serapis was represented as a bearded god, seated and wearing a modius (grain measure) on his head. All in all, he looked very much like Hades or Zeus. To Greek worshipers, his personality and powers were a combination of the ones possessed by those two gods, with elements of Helios, Asclepius, and Dionysus. Like Zeus, Serapis was associated with ruling; like Helios, he represented the sun;

like Hades, he was a god of the underworld; and, like Dionysus, he was god of fertility and renewal. He is connected with Asclepius because both had the power of healing. In his modified form, Serapis quickly became popular beyond the Nile Valley in a way that the more obviously Egyptian Osiris could not have done. The image of Serapis as the consort of Isis survived and spread to Rome. Today, however, it is again Serapis who is the less well known god, while images of Osiris are commonly displayed in art books and on tourist souvenirs of Egypt.

Abydos

When Isis had reassembled the body of Osiris, it was buried at Abydos in the low desert west of the Nile River, which, according to tradition, is where Seth killed him. Abydos became a prominent sacred city, a royal necropolis of the first two dynasties, and an important place of pilgrimage. Archaeological excavations in the late 19th century CE revealed that the original tutelary deity of Abydos had been the jackal god Khenti-amentiu, but that his cult had gradually been absorbed by that of Osiris. Egyptians wanted to be buried as close as possible to the tomb of Osiris, but only the richest of them could afford it. For the rest, stelae were set up, inscribed with the dead person's name and titles and a prayer to the god. Thousands of these stelae have been found in the cemeteries of Abydos.

Below: Dating from between 1500 and 1000 BCE, this painting shows Osiris in front of a boat carrying a beetle, which symbolizes the sun.

The temple of Osiris at Abydos was successively rebuilt or enlarged from the 24th century BCE until the reign of Ahmoze II (570–526 BCE). Some pharaohs had a cenotaph or a mortuary temple there. The temple of Seti I (reigned 1318–1304 BCE) was one of the most beautiful of all such temples. Behind it is a structure known as the Osirion. Dedicated to Osiris, as its name suggests, it was probably Seti's cenotaph. It comprises an underground vaulted hall containing a central platform with 10 monolithic pillars surrounded by a channel of water.

LYN GREEN

Above: On the lower part of this sandstone stele is Ounennefer, high priest of Osiris during the reign of Ramses II (1304–1237 BCE), with his wife and parents. Above them are the deities (left to right) Hathor, Horus, Osiris, and Isis.

Bibliography

Faulkner, Raymond, trans. *The Egyptian Book of the Dead.* San Francisco: Chronicle Books, 2000.

Spence, Lewis. *Ancient Egyptian Myths and Legends.* New York: Dover Publications, 1991.

SEE ALSO: Anubis; Egypt; Geb; Horus; Isis; Nepthys; Nut; Seth.

PAEON

Paeon was an early god of healing sometimes called "the physician of the gods," to whom he ministered on Mount Olympus. However, there are relatively few references to Paeon in classical literature, and very little is known of what were thought to be his character and attributes.

There are passing allusions to Paeon in the *Argonautica* of Alexandrian poet Apollonius of Rhodes (third century BCE), where the name is used as a byword for skill in healing. He is also mentioned in the *Odes*, by another Greek poet, Pindar (c. 522–c. 438 BCE), and the *Dionysiaca* by Nonnus (fl. c. 450–470 CE), an account of a journey by the god Dionysus to India. However, Paeon is written about at greatest length by Homer (c. ninth–eighth century BCE) in the *Iliad*, an account of the 10-year war between the Greeks and the Trojans. According to Homer, after Hades, the god of the underworld, was shot by one of Heracles' arrows, he fled to Mount Olympus to seek the help of Zeus. He was healed by Paeon, who treated the wound with soothing herbs.

Later, when the god Ares entered the war on the side of the Trojans, he was wounded in battle by Greek hero Diomedes. Aided by the goddess Athena, Diomedes thrust a spear into Ares' stomach. Like Hades before him, Ares retreated to Mount Olympus. Zeus then told Paeon to treat the war god's wound. Homer tells us that Ares' wound was healed the moment that Paeon's herbs touched it.

Some classicists believe that Paeon can be identified with Asclepius, the son of Apollo, who became the major god of medicine in the world of antiquity. The name Paeon itself is of obscure origin, although some scholars believe it derives from the name of the Cretan god Paiawon, who was mentioned in inscriptions at the palace of Knossos. Paiawon, however, was a god of war, not of healing, and any link between the two figures remains unexplained.

Other Paeons

In addition to the god of healing, there were several other figures in classical mythology named Paeon. One was a Trojan mentioned in Homer's enumeration of the forces of Troy. He was the husband of Cleomede and father of Agastrophus and Laophoon. Another Paeon was the king of Messenia, son of Antilochus and grandson of Nestor. A third Paeon was the son of Endymion. He lost a footrace at Olympia against his brother Epeius and went into exile in the region of Macedonia known as Paeonia.

PETER CONNOR

Right: This marble statuette from around 400–200 BCE depicts the Greek god of medicine Asclepius, with whom Paeon was often identified.

Bibliography
Bulfinch, Thomas. *Bulfinch's Mythology*. New York: Modern Library, 1998.
Homer, and Robert Fagles, trans. *The Iliad*. New York: Penguin USA, 2003.

SEE ALSO: Ares; Asclepius; Crete; Diomedes; Dionysus; Endymion; Heracles; Zeus.

PAGANISM

Paganism has come to mean any religion other than Judaism, Christianity, and Islam. However, the English word *pagan* derives from Latin *pagus*, "countryside." Ancient Romans used the term to refer to religions practiced by people from outside Rome, especially country folk.

During the Roman Empire, which lasted from 30 BCE to 476 CE, many exotic and alien religions found their way into Rome from outlying parts of its far-flung territories. Religions from the eastern frontiers were especially remarkable for their radical differences from the polytheistic religion of native Romans. Among them were Mithraism, a mystery religion that originated in Persia; and the cult of Cybele, a goddess of Asia Minor whose male devotees castrated themselves and dressed in women's clothing. The most important was Christianity, an offshoot of Judaism that originated in Palestine and spread through the urban centers of the empire, where it first appealed to women, slaves, and other disenfranchised members of society.

Although Christianity was pagan in the ancient Roman sense of the term, because it came from outside the city of Rome, it cannot be so described in modern English. Today, in order to merit the term *pagan*, a religion must be practiced by no more than a small minority within a society; in addition, it must be regarded as eccentric by the conventional majority. The religions that were regarded as pagan by the Romans, and which may still be so described today, are those that evolved during the Bronze and Iron Ages anywhere other than in Rome itself and which were superseded or assimilated by Roman forms of worship. They include the religions of the Apuli, Brutii, Calabri, Campani, Etrusci, Galli, Histri, Latini, Liguri, Lucani, Piceni, Samniti, Sabini, Umbri, and Veneti. Since most of these peoples did not leave extensive written records, much of what is known about them comes from archaeological finds and from comments made about them by later Roman writers. The best documented early religions are those of the Apuli, Etrusci, Umbri, and Veneti.

Divination and augury

In many early religions, divination and augury—reading the future in omens—were important components of the priest's role, but Italian paganism was especially concerned with these practices. The Etruscans—people from the region of central Italy surrounding the modern city of

Left: Pagan Mithraism survived in Rome even after the advent of Christianity. This bas-relief of Mithras dates from the second century CE.

The Changing Meanings of *Paganism*

For Romans, the term *paganism* had a slightly derogatory meaning—it referred to the religion of people who were regarded as country bumpkins. Rural religion was often highly localized, while urban religion could lay claim to more important and universal cults. When Christianity began to spread throughout the Roman Empire, it first took hold in the cities, gradually ousting not only the previously established religion but also other cults that were, like itself, imported. The country folk, more removed from the political and religious turmoil of the cities, quietly continued to worship as they always had. By the fall of the Roman Empire in the fifth century CE, the previous contrast between rural and urban religion—which had largely been a question of the richness of temples, the political importance of priests, and the benefits that worship of a deity was believed to offer—had turned into a contrast between paganism and Christianity. After Christianity became the dominant religion of all of Europe, the rural connotations of *paganism* were overwritten by connotations of unenlightened polytheism. In extreme cases, pagans were persecuted as heretics. Nonetheless, after 15 centuries of dominance, in the 19th and 20th centuries Christianity began to lose some of its attraction for small but significant groups of Westerners who began to seek new forms of religious expression. They formed neopagan groups and adopted ancient beliefs. Followers of Asatru, for example, still adhere to pre-Christian Norse religion.

Above: Dogon people of Mali perform a divination ritual using footprints left in the sand by a jackal.

Florence—were particularly known for their preoccupation with signs and portents. In the view of Roman philosopher, statesman, and dramatist Seneca (c. 4 BCE–65 CE), the difference between Romans and Etruscans was that, while Romans believed that "lightning flashes give an indication of the future because they are produced, [Etruscans believed] that they are produced because they have something to indicate." In the Etruscan view, everything occurred because it was the will of the gods, and every occurrence was a message from the gods that humans ignored at their peril. While Romans and Etruscans both divined the future by interpreting lightning and reading signs in the viscera (innards), especially the liver, of sacrificed animals, Romans' favored form was ornithomancy—reading portents in the flight of birds.

Pagan foundation myths

While many cultures and religions have creation myths that account for the origin of the universe, some have legends that describe the establishment of their principal settlement. For example, the Umbrians believed that their ancestors were exiles who had followed an animal to their eventual place of settlement in the valley of the Tiber River north of Rome in central Italy. This idea was later adopted by the Romans themselves and turned into a rite known as *Ver Sacrum*, or "Sacred Spring." After a disaster such as a plague, a war, or a crisis of overpopulation, people would dedicate all living things born in a certain year to the god Mars, who was himself probably adapted from the earlier pre-Roman deity Mavors. In March, Mars's month, livestock would be sacrificed and the men of arms-bearing age would leave their native town, following an animal that had also been dedicated to Mars, until it stopped, lay down, or otherwise indicated that this was the place for the humans to start a new community. The exiled group took a new name from the animal that had led them. Thus the Piceni were so called because they had been brought to their adopted region by a woodpecker (*picus*); the Hirpini by a wolf (*hirpus*); the Ursenti by a bear (*ursus*).

Some Etruscan Divinities

Deity	Roman Counterpart	Greek Counterpart	Responsibility/Attributes
Apulu	Apollo	Apollo	sun, healing
Artums	Diana	Artemis	the moon
Fufluns	Bacchus	Dionysus	wine
Hercle	Hercules	Heracles	deified, mortal-born hero
Maris	Mars	Ares	war and warriors
Menerva	Minerva	Athena	wisdom
Nethuns	Neptune	Poseidon	sea
Phersipnai	Proserpina	Persephone	queen of the dead
Satres	Saturn	Uranus	heaven, agriculture
Selvans	Sylvanus	Pan	forest, woodland fields, cattle
Sethlans	Vulcan	Hephaestus	fire, blacksmiths
Tin/Tinia	Jupiter/Jove	Zeus	principal sky god, thunderbolts
Turan	Venus	Aphrodite	love and sex
Turms	Mercury	Hermes	travel, communication, commerce
Uni	Juno	Hera	maternity, marriage
Vetis	Vedius	Hades	underworld

Seven bronze tablets known as the Iguvine Tablets describe the religious rituals of the Umbrians of Iguvium (modern Gubbio). Their general pattern of worship consisted of taking auguries from the flight of birds, ritual purification, a prayer establishing a pact or relationship with the deity in question, and a sacrifice or offering to clinch the deal. Ceremonies might be public, such as rituals to expiate the community's sins and purify the city and its acropolis, or private, such as sacrifices to ward off bad luck. Offerings might take the form of wine, cakes, grain, or fat, while sacrifices consisted of animals—cattle, pigs, sheep, or dogs—carefully chosen for their color, sex, age, and breeding as appropriate for the particular ritual and the deities involved.

From the earliest times, Italian deities had two names—one by which they were generally identified, another that depended on the role they were playing or where they were at a particular time. The Romans adopted this custom. For example, when the god of war was taking revenge, he was known as Mars Ulltor (the Avenger). Diana was worshiped at the Latin town of Aricia, near Lake Nemi, which is known as "Diana's mirror." When the goddess was there, she was known as Diana Nemorensis

Left: This relief depicts Emperor Marcus Aurelius (ruled 161–180 CE) making a sacrifice at the Temple of Jupiter.

Above: Etruscans were among the many ancient pagan peoples who attached great mystical significance to lightning.

(Diana of Nemi). Thus Roman gods and goddesses ended up with numerous names. Juno, for example, was variously Juno Lucina (Juno Who Gives Birth), Juno Regina (Juno the Queen), or Juno Moneta (Juno the Warner). This pattern is seen even in the religion of the non-Indo-European Etruscans, suggesting that it is a characteristic that developed in Italy rather than an Indo-European inheritance. The Romans continued this naming system as they encountered other ethnic groups in the expansion of the empire; thus, the Celtic Sulis, goddess of the hot springs at Bath, England, was associated with Minerva and known as Sulis Minerva.

Later pagan practices

Christianity eventually wiped out paganism, but vestigial beliefs and practices lingered on into the Middle Ages. In *De Ecclesiasticis Disciplinus*, German monk Regino von Prüm (d. c. 915 CE) wrote of women who "believe and declare that they can ride with Diana the pagan goddess and a huge throng of women on chosen beasts in the hours of night. They say that in the silence of the night they can traverse great stretches of territory, that they obey Diana as though she were their special mistress, and that on certain nights she calls them to her special service."

In the 19th century CE, the Romantic movement in art and literature inspired a pagan revival, particularly of druids in Britain. In the 20th century several spiritual movements attempted to revive ancient polytheistic religions of Europe and western Asia. Although today opponents of such practices denounce them as a form of witchcraft, modern paganism is concerned with authentic pantheons and rituals of ancient cultures. Such revivalist, or neopagan, religions base their rituals on changes of the seasons and the personification of nature, and are thus particularly attractive to people with strong ecological concerns.

The following are some of the most popular pagan groups today: the Church of All Worlds, adherents of which worship the earth mother goddess; Feraferia ("Wilderness Sacrament"), which is based on worship of ancient Greek goddesses; Pagan Way, a nature religion that venerates earth goddesses and the seasons; the Reformed Druids of North America; the Church of the Eternal Source, which has revived ancient Egyptian religion; and the Viking Brotherhood, which celebrates Norse rites. Since the late 1970s, some feminists have revived certain forms of witchcraft and paganism.

LESLIE ELLEN JONES

Bibliography

Bulfinch, Thomas. *Bulfinch's Mythology.* New York: Modern Library, 1998.

Ellis, Peter Berresford. *A Brief History of the Druids.* New York: Carroll and Graf, 2002.

Howatson, M. C., and Ian Chilvers. *Concise Oxford Companion to Classical Literature.* New York: Oxford University Press, 1993.

Willis, Roy, ed. *World Mythology: The Illustrated Guide.* New York: Simon and Schuster, 1993.

SEE ALSO: Celts; Druids; Earth Mother; Mars; Mithraism; Nature Religions; Rome; Scandinavia.

PAN

Pan, the shepherd god usually depicted playing upon his pipes, is one of the most instantly recognizable of the Greek gods. As well as his musical abilities, he was also famous for the fear (or "panic") that he was able to inspire in people.

Pan's familiarity in the modern world is reflected in the fact that he was both the inspiration for James M. Barrie's Peter Pan and a model for the depictions of Satan in medieval art. At that time in European history, the lusty earthiness and supposed brutishness of the Arcadian shepherd deity stood in sharp contrast to the Christian notion of what "a good shepherd" should be. The goat-man's very appearance suggested "lower forces" like sexual instincts and raw emotions. With his hairy nudity, horns, pointed ears, and hooves, Pan became a figure of satanic evil. The ancient Greeks saw Pan quite differently—neither eternally boyish nor a devil.

Family background

According to the Homeric "Hymn to Pan," the author of which is unknown, the god was the son of Hermes, messenger of the Greek gods, and an unnamed daughter of the nymph Dryope. Like Hermes, Pan was known for his cunning and fleet-footedness. Both Hermes and Pan were associated with Arcadia, a region in the central Peloponnese known for its forests and wild, mountainous terrain. Pan was part man and part goat. Although his exact composition varied, he was usually depicted as having the legs and cloven hooves of a goat and the upper body of a man. However, a pair of horns protruded from his human head. Pan's association with the goat was connected to the terrain of his homeland—much of Arcadia was too mountainous for sheep and cattle, and only goats could survive there.

Other sources give different accounts of Pan's parentage. According to one, Pan was the result of a liaison between Zeus, the king of the gods, and Penelope, the wife of the Greek hero Odysseus. A rarer legend makes him the magical offspring of a shepherd named Crathis and a she-goat.

The Homeric "Hymn to Pan" says that Pan was given his name because he brought joy to the hearts of all the Greek gods—*pan* is the Greek word for "all." Because of this connection, some scholars have suggested that Pan was in some way a cosmic god who could be identified with the whole universe. However, most scholars believe that it is more likely that Pan's name is derived from the same root as the Latin word *pasco*, meaning "feeder" or "shepherd."

A creature of the night

Although artists have often depicted Pan playing his pipes and dancing with nymphs in sunny meadows, most classical sources say that he lived a nocturnal existence. Greek poet Theocritus (c. 310–250 BCE) tells us he became touchy and cranky in the midday sun. Because the hot, draining sun depressed Pan, he escaped by sleeping in shady groves. He favored those who slept at the same

Left: This statue depicts Pan playing the panpipes or syrinx, the musical instrument that became his most famous attribute.

time, even giving them secret knowledge. Pan healed, too, appearing in the noontime dreams of others to heal a dying child or to impart crucial information. However, when noisy humans accidentally or intentionally interrupted Pan's midday sleep, he flew into a violent rage. Then he would project an overwhelming sense of fear that would afflict anyone within a certain range. This sensation was known to the ancient Greeks as "panic" (see box, page 1076).

Many of the myths about Pan revolve around his attempts at seduction, which involved goddesses, nymphs, and mortal women. These attempts were usually unsuccessful. One of the few exceptions was his pursuit of Selene, the goddess of the moon. There are various accounts of Pan's seduction of her. One says that he lured her into the woods by disguising himself in a silky fleece of white wool; another says that he persuaded Selene to engage in a brief affair by giving her a herd of white oxen. The implication of these stories is that Selene found the god too ugly and ungainly to warrant her attentions without being tricked or bribed.

Pitys and Echo

Most of the objects of Pan's attentions were nymphs. One nymph who suffered because of Pan's love for her was Pitys. Like most of those he pursued, Pitys found Pan hideously unattractive and fled from him when he approached her. She was then turned into a pine tree. In a tribute to her memory, Pan often wore a crown of pine sprays or carried a pine branch. Another version of this myth says that Pitys was loved by both Pan and Boreas, the god of the north wind. In a fit of jealously Boreas blew her off the top of a cliff. In pity, the earth goddess Gaia transformed her into a pine tree at the point where she fell.

Another nymph who was unfortunate enough to attract the attention of Pan was Echo. There are various myths associated with her, all of which attempt to explain the phenomenon of echoing. While the most famous involve the goddess Hera and the beautiful mortal Narcissus, a third has Pan as a central character. As in the myth of Pan and Pitys, the central theme is Pan's unrequited love. Echo rejected all of Pan's advances and fled when he pursued her. Infuriated by his failure, Pan used his powers to make a group of shepherds crazed with desire. Unlike the god, they found a way to capture the poor nymph and brutally dismembered her until only her voice remained.

Another version of the myth has a less violent ending. It says that Echo bore Pan a daughter named Iambe. Iambe was associated with a two-syllable poetic phrase or meter called an iamb—a term familiar to all students who study

Horned Gods

Pan's characteristic horns, beard, and love for music and dance link him to nature gods from many other ancient cultures. Scholars such as archaeologist Marija Gimbutas (1921–1994) have linked Pan to images of a prehistoric horned god that date from the Upper Paleolithic period (c. 40,000–10,000 BCE). Cave paintings found in France and Spain show a strange figure, sometimes known as the Master of Animals or God of Wild Nature, wearing bison or stag horns, apparently performing a ritual dance. In classical and later times, related horned figures appeared. They include not only Pan and his Roman equivalents Faunus and Silvanus, but also the Celtic god Cernunnos, the Russian Leshy and Vidassus, the Scandinavian Rå, the Welsh Merlin, the Lithuanian Ganiklis, and many others.

Like Pan, these divine guardians of animals and nature were said to have eerie voices and considerable powers of prophecy. By historical times, these ancient figures had become mysterious shepherd-gods of forests and remote mountainous regions. Their hold on human imagination was so strong that they were never in danger of becoming extinct, however. For example, Pan had more than a hundred cult sites where he was worshiped in ancient Greece, an indication of his importance to ordinary people.

Above: Scholars believe that the Celtic god Cernunnos is related to Pan. This depiction of the horned deity is found on the Gundestrup Cauldron, a silver vessel dating from the second century BCE.

Panic

Pan was known for his ability to inspire sudden and irrational fear in people—the sensation we know today as panic. Most of the stories in which Pan unleashed this power involve military conflicts. The most famous is that of the Battle of Marathon, which was fought between the Athenians and the Persians in 490 BCE. Legend has it that Pan appeared before the Athenian messenger Pheidippides in the mountains and asked him why the people of his city did not worship him. Pan said that he had helped the Athenians in the past and would do so again. True to his word, Pan came to the aid of the Athenian army at Marathon. In gratitude the Athenians dedicated a shrine to him on the slopes of the Acropolis.

The Battle of Marathon was only one instance when Pan was said to have helped Athenian or Greek forces. In many cases the battle in question was said to have taken place close to one of the god's sanctuaries or caves. In 480 BCE, during the second Persian War, the Greeks defeated Xerxes' fleet near Psyttaleia, an island sacred to Pan. In 403 BCE at Piraeus, the army of the Thirty Tyrants was said to have been overtaken by panic when a heavy snowstorm fell out of a clear sky at midday—again, a cave sacred to Pan was nearby.

Below: This illustration from a sarcophagus depicts a scene from the Battle of Marathon. According to legend, the god Pan intervened on behalf of the Athenians, spreading panic in the Persian ranks.

poetry. This daughter of Pan is also famous for her rough wit, which restored laughter to a grieving Demeter and thereby brought fertility back to the earth. Yet another myth has Pan and Echo producing a daughter named Iynx. She became famous for her ability to work love charms. Her best-known spell attracted Zeus to Io, an act that led to Io's being turned into a bird by Zeus's wife Hera. The idea that the unlucky-in-love Pan could father a daughter who could make people fall in love at will is particularly ironic.

Syrinx and the pipes of Pan

Pan's most famous involvement was with the tree spirit Syrinx. Their story is recorded by Roman poet Ovid (43 BCE–17 CE) in his *Metamorphoses*. Pan fell deeply in love with Syrinx, but she fled from him, just as Pitys and Echo had done. Syrinx was frightened that Pan would rape her,

so she ran until she reached the Ladon River, where Pan caught her. At this point she prayed to the river nymphs to save her. Syrinx was immediately transformed into a bunch of reeds. As Pan held the reeds in his arms, the wind blew through them, producing a haunting note. Enchanted by the noise, Pan cut the reeds to different lengths and bound them together, producing what would come to be known as a set of panpipes. The instrument's Greek name, however, is the *syrinx*.

Scholars have put various interpretations on the myths involving Pan's tragic attempts at seduction. Some have suggested that the myths highlight the impossibility of "owning" what belongs to nature. Even a god such as Pan has to respect these boundaries. Pan's lustful nature compels him to attempt to seize the nymphs—personifications of aspects of the natural world—but these efforts simply lead to destruction and grief.

Above: Pan and Psyche *by Edward Burne-Jones (1833–1898). The shepherd god is depicted comforting the nymph after the loss of her lover Eros. While most myths involving Pan revolve around his lustful pursuit of a nymph, the story of Pan and Psyche highlights a gentler side of his nature.*

Pan the musician

Pan's set of pipes became his most famous attribute—in art he is almost always depicted with the instrument. In the ancient world he was renowned for his musicianship. In one myth, Pan competed with the god Apollo in a musical contest (although in some variants, the competition was between Apollo and the satyr Marsyas). Pan had earlier boasted that the god's skill was inferior to his own. The judge was the mountain god Tmolus. Apollo played on a lyre inlaid with gems and ivory, an ornate instrument that contrasted sharply with the crude pipes that Pan played upon. Tmolus was entranced by the god's music and declared the sun god the victor. However, Tmolus was not the only person to overhear the contest. Midas, king of Phrygia, was also listening. Midas, famous for his greed and lack of refinement, preferred the simpler, rustic sounds of Pan's music and said so. Apollo was so angry that he changed Midas's ears into asses' ears, a visible sign of his lack of taste.

Not all of the myths attached to Pan show him in a bad light. For example, the myth of Pan and Psyche shows his benevolent side. Psyche was the lover of the god Eros, who visited her in the hours of darkness so that she could not see him. When she discovered his true identity, he left her. Psyche was distraught by this loss and tried to drown herself because of her despair. Pan found her near death among the herbs on a riverbank. Remembering his own agony after losing Syrinx in the reeds of the Ladon River, he comforted Psyche and persuaded her to attempt to win back her lover.

The worship of Pan

Greek historian Herodotus (c. 484–425 BCE) says that the Greeks first worshiped Pan around 800 years before the historian was born—that is to say, in the 13th century BCE. Other classical literary sources suggest that Pan was first worshiped in Arcadia, the mountainous area of the Peloponnese where he was believed to have lived. The Greek travel writer Pausanias (143–176 CE) names several sites in the region sacred to the god. He tells of a bronze statue of the god at Megalopolis, and also mentions a stone image of Pan at the town's temple to Zeus. Pausanias also writes about several other sanctuaries to Pan in the area: one at Mount Lycaeus, another in the Nomia mountains, and one on the road from Tegea to Laconia. Pausanias also says that on Mount Parthenios there were tortoises whose shells were ideal for making lyres. However, the local inhabitants were afraid to kill the tortoises because they believed that they were sacred to Pan.

Pan is widely depicted in both classical and more modern art. Illustrations of ancient Greek drinking cups show Pan plucking grapes and carrying wineskins. The story of Pan's attempt to seduce Syrinx has been a popular subject for later artists. It is captured by Flemish artist Jacob Jordaens (1593–1678) in his 1625 painting *Pan and Syrinx*; by Nicolas Poussin (1594–1665) in *Nymph Syrinx Pursued by Pan*; and by Alessandro Turchi (1578–1649) in *Pan and the Nymph Syrinx*. Pan's attempt to soothe Psyche, meanwhile, is the subject of a painting by Edward Burne-Jones (1833–1898), *Pan and Psyche*.

KATHLEEN JENKS

Below: This Roman statue depicts Pan showing the herdsman Daphnis how to play the pipes. Later, Daphnis was blinded by a jealous nymph and spent the rest of his life singing mournful songs about his tragic fate.

Bibliography

Crudden, Michael, trans. *The Homeric Hymns*. New York: Oxford University Press, 2002.

Ovid, and A. D. Melville, trans. *Metamorphoses*. New York: Oxford University Press, 1998.

Pausanias, and Peter Levi, trans. *Guide to Greece*. New York: Viking Press, 1984.

SEE ALSO: Apollo; Celts; Echo; Eros; Faunus; Hermes; Midas; Psyche; Zeus.

PANDORA

In Greek mythology, Pandora is the first woman, a beautiful but problematic creature designed by the gods as a punishment for mortal men. Traditionally, curiosity compels Pandora to open a jar containing all kinds of ills and suffering, freeing the afflictions on humankind.

The principal accounts of the myth of Pandora are found in two works by Greek poet Hesiod (fl. 800 BCE), *Theogony* and *Works and Days*. While both versions have much in common, there are also many significant differences. *Theogony* gives her no name, but in *Works and Days* the name Pandora and its etymology play a central role. Pandora is sometimes compared to Eve from the Book of Genesis in the Bible, another first woman whose curiosity leads to trouble for humans. The problems that arose from Pandora's curiosity have become proverbial, giving rise to the common expression *to open a Pandora's box.*

In *Theogony*, which recounts the births of the gods, the creation or invention of humans requires no explanation. Although female divinities exist from the beginning of time, the first mortals are assumed to be male. Scholars of Greek mythology suggest that, because men were fashioned to appear like the gods and because asexual reproduction occurs among the gods, female partners for men were unnecessary. Unlike the account given in the Book of

Below: In Eva Prima Pandora, *French painter Jean Cousin the Elder (1490–1560) compares the biblical figure of Eve to Pandora, the first woman in Greek mythology. Her left hand rests on a jar that she will eventually open, releasing suffering into the world.*

Genesis, where woman is created as man's companion, here woman is created as a source of woe for man. In each case the creation of woman is the beginning of human marriage, but in *Theogony* this too is presented as an evil. Hesiod held a pessimistic view of human existence that led him to conclude that children are more a burden than a cause for rejoicing. He likewise undervalued other female contributions to the family. Rather than offering physical and emotional companionship, contributing to the household resources, and bearing children, Hesiod declared that woman is a drain on resources, whose curiosity causes disaster.

In Hesiod the first woman is created by Hephaestus, god of fire and metalworking, who molds her out of clay. In this way she is like Adam in the Book of Genesis, who is also made from the earth, but unlike Eve, who is fashioned from Adam's body. The Greek woman is made at the command of Zeus, chief of the gods, not to complete human existence, but as a punishment for mortals because

Below: Spanish artist Diego Rodriguez (1599–1660) depicts the god Apollo visiting the forge of Roman god Vulcan (Hephaestus in Greek mythology). In this smithy, Pandora is fashioned from clay.

they were enjoying the benefits of the gift of fire given to them by the Titan Prometheus. Womankind is only one of a series of deceitful gifts given to mortal men in the lengthy conflict involving Prometheus and Zeus.

Hesiod's version of the myth

The story of the gods' feud is most fully recounted in *Theogony,* in which Prometheus, although divine, is a protector of mortals. The conflict begins when he sets out a sacrifice to Zeus and divides the portions unequally into meat and bones wrapped in fat. Since Zeus knows all things, it is doubtful he was truly deceived, but he takes the bones and leaves the meat for mortals, thus setting the sacrificial protocol for all time. Angered by Prometheus's trick, Zeus denies mortals the use of fire, but Prometheus endeavors to steal it and return it to them. To achieve this end, Prometheus travels to Mount Olympus and takes a glowing charcoal from a torch. Securing it in a large stalk of fennel, he smuggles it back to the mortal world. In exchange for this insult, Zeus decides to create an inescapable evil for men and commands the gods to make woman. Hephaestus fashions her from the earth using clay, while Athena, goddess of war and handicrafts, dresses and

adorns her. Hesiod notes that the "race of women" is descended from the gods' creation and that she brings trouble to men, but he adds that any man who avoids marriage will also suffer from the lack of children to care for him in his old age and to inherit his property. This is known among scholars of Greek mythology as the "misogynist's dilemma" and is considered to be a major factor in the Pandora myth, which makes the evils brought by women truly "inescapable."

A longer account of the myth in *Works and Days* lists the gifts given to the woman by each god: she is dressed and adorned by Athena, the Graces, Persuasion, and the Hours; while Hermes, messenger of the gods, gives her a deceitful nature and teaches her to lie. In some versions of the myth the final gift, given by Zeus, is a jar that she is instructed not to open; in other versions the jar belongs to Epimetheus or Prometheus. Zeus then names the first woman Pandora, "All gifts," because each of the gods gave her a gift. Epimetheus ("Afterthought"), the dim-witted brother of Prometheus ("Forethought"), accepts the gift of woman despite his brother's warnings and marries Pandora. Until then men had lived lives of ease. However, once Pandora released diseases and toil from the jar,

The Role of Hope

The most puzzling aspect of the Pandora myth is the role of hope, alone left in the jar after all the evils have flown. Various interpretations of the myth have tried to determine if hope brightens the otherwise grim picture of human life, if it remains inaccessible because it is trapped in the jar, or if it is an evil that prevents mortals from seeing things clearly.

A later version of the myth, told by second-century-BCE Greek writer Babrius in his collection of fables, offers a different interpretation. In this version Zeus gathers all good elements and, placing them in a jar with a lid, leaves them among humans. They are unable to contain their curiosity and open the jar, at which point all the good things fly away, leaving only hope. Here the culprit is not a woman but a generic human being (*anthropos*). While there is still a moral message in this version, it emphasizes human folly but is less pessimistic than Hesiod's account.

Below: In this painting by German artist Johann Heiss (1660–1704), the Roman god Vulcan (Hephaestus) presents the naked first woman Pandora to the Roman god Jupiter (Zeus).

Left: This illustration by English artist Arthur Rackham (1867–1939) depicts Pandora as an innocent girl opening a box, which sets free all kinds of evil into the world.

Pandora's name

There are various interpretations of the meaning of Pandora's name. Hesiod explains that it means "she who is given all gifts." In other accounts Pandora is an epithet of the goddess Gaia, the earth, who is the source of all life for mortals, "she who gives all gifts." This interpretation is reinforced by an image on an Attic vase depicting the creation of woman, which labels the central figure *Anesidora,* which unambiguously means "she who sends up gifts [from the earth]."

The ambiguity of Pandora's name can be interpreted in either of two ways. One possibility is that the divine epithet indicates that Pandora was originally a goddess. This type of explanation was popular when scholars of Greek religion believed that all mythic figures were based on deities whose power had faded. Another interpretation considers what the myth suggests about the valuation of women. Some scholars have argued that Hesiod's rejection of women's contributions to human existence points to a desire to obscure the degree to which men actually depended on them. The ambiguous nature of the name has continued to shape the reception of Pandora throughout the centuries. She can stand for good or evil, depending on whether the myth or the meaning of the name is given prominence.

Pandora is not mentioned by name in either of the epic poems of Homer (c. ninth–eighth century BCE), the *Iliad* or the *Odyssey,* but she serves as Homer's model for the mythological figure Helen, wife of Menelaus, king of Sparta. Scholars argue that when Paris carries Helen from Sparta at the urging of the goddess Aphrodite, and when the old men of Troy say that there is no shame in risking everything for so beautiful a woman, they collectively assume the role of a latter-day Epimetheus deceived into accepting a treacherous and ruinous gift. Pandora does not play a large role in later Greek literature, although there are traces in other myths of the misogynistic attitude found in Hesiod's record of her myth.

Changing representations of Pandora

Since classical times representations of Pandora have adorned various vases and appeared on different buildings. The importance of the myth for classical Athens is demonstrated by Greek travel writer Pausanias (143–176 CE), who reports that the creation of Pandora was depicted

men's lives became miserable, and the world became a place that was hard to tolerate. However, one element remained in the jar after the other miseries had escaped: hope. Although there are many interpretations of the myth that attempt to explain why hope remained, there is no conclusive reason.

Pandora's jar also hints at the part of women's role that Hesiod criticizes. The word *pithos,* used for the jar, indicates a large jar used for long-term storage of grains and other necessities, but *pithos* can have another meaning. The belly of the jar can also represent a womb, and thus the evils that Pandora brings forth are her offspring. This pessimistic reading is in keeping with Hesiod's largely negative attitude toward childbearing.

on the base of the famous statue of Athena Parthenos in the Parthenon on the Acropolis. The myth of a first woman made of clay was of special interest to the Athenians, who claimed to be autochthonous (born from the earth of Attica). Few if any images from antiquity show Pandora with a jar; the often repeated image of Pandora lifting the lid of a box rather than a jar to let out the evil contents dates only from the Renaissance (c. 1375–c. 1575).

Roman authors had little to say about Pandora. It was the fathers of the Christian church in the late Roman Empire (30 BCE–476 CE) who first equated Pandora with Eve, a comparison that was to have a lasting impact on Western culture. Tertullian (c. 155 or 160–after 220 CE) uses Pandora as both a positive and a negative figure, while for Greek prelate Gregory of Nazianzus (c. 330–c. 389 CE) she exemplifies vanity, unhealthy curiosity, and other negative traits. Greek Christian writer and teacher Origen (c.185–254 CE) explicitly compares the *pithos* or jar with the forbidden fruit in the garden of Eden. He was familiar with Hesiod's version of the Pandora myth, which he ridicules while quoting it at length. English poet John Milton (1608–1674) also compared Eve to Pandora in his poem *Paradise Lost* and in other writings.

The myth of Pandora has given English and many other languages the phrase *Pandora's box*. In the book *Pandora's Box* (1961), American art historians Erwin (1892–1968) and Dora (d. 1965) Panofsky detail how the figure of Pandora became associated with a box that does not appear in ancient art or in ancient literature. They trace this change to the great Dutch humanist Erasmus of Rotterdam (c. 1466–1536), who used the myth to illustrate the perils of "becoming a wise man too late." Erasmus turned the *pithos* into a *pyxis*, a small box or casket, a change that has had a great influence on the iconography of the Pandora myth. In his account, Erasmus drew upon a version of the myth attributed to Greek poet Philodemus (c. 110–c. 35 BCE), which stated that Epimetheus rather than Pandora opened the box.

By the 16th century Pandora was described as a mixture of good and evil, which allowed French poets Pierre Ronsard (1524–1585) and Joachim du Bellay

(c. 1522–1560) to use her in their poetry. Ronsard compares Pandora to a beloved lady, while du Bellay compares her to the ambiguous city of Rome, a city that is not always kind to its inhabitants. The city of Paris was represented as a "New Pandora," which only gave out good things, in contrast to the ambiguous city of Rome, the "Old Pandora." As the century progressed, however, even the "Old" Pandora was redeemed and the meaning of her name came to stand for all good things. *Pandora* was even used as an honorific title for Queen Elizabeth I of England, along with the more familiar *Gloriana*.

The myth of Pandora was also popular with dramatists of the 17th and 18th centuries, from Spanish playwright Calderón (1799–1867) to French writer Voltaire (1694–1778) and German poet Goethe (1749–1832), all of whom took great liberties with the myth while using it

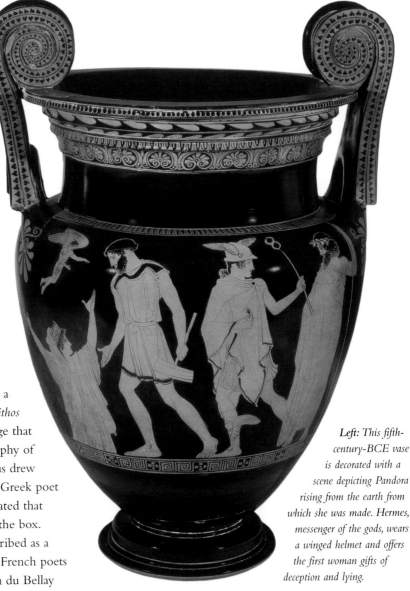

Left: This fifth-century-BCE vase is decorated with a scene depicting Pandora rising from the earth from which she was made. Hermes, messenger of the gods, wears a winged helmet and offers the first woman gifts of deception and lying.

to explore a variety of philosophical issues. In plays by these writers, Pandora is respectively a creation of Prometheus representing science and art, a frail woman enthralled by love, and a divine bringer of peace and beauty to human beings.

In the early 19th century, English artist John Flaxman (1755–1826) painted a series of images illustrating a translation of Hesiod that adhered closely to the myth, although it omitted some of the harsher details in order to turn Pandora into a more admirable figure. English pre-Raphaelite artist Dante Gabriel Rossetti (1828–1882) painted a number of versions of Pandora, depicting her as an intense-looking young woman holding down the lid of a casket with great concentration.

Below: While early versions of the Pandora myth recount that she opens a jar full of evil, later the vessel was often described as a box. English artist Dante Gabriel Rossetti's impression of Pandora depicts her clutching a box, from which issues a plume of evil smoke.

Other Pandoras, Other Creation Myths

The name *Pandora*, as well as being an epithet of Gaia, the earth, is also given to several other minor figures in Greek mythology. One is a daughter of the legendary Athenian king Erechtheus, who together with her sister sacrifices herself for the benefit of the city. Another Pandora has an intriguing connection to the theme of human origins. She is the mother of Graecus, whom the Greeks were named for, and either the daughter or the wife of Deucalion, son of Prometheus. Deucalion is usually said to be married to Pyrrha, the daughter of his brother Epimetheus. After Zeus floods the earth to punish human misdeeds, Deucalion and Pyrrha, the sole survivors, are told to repopulate the earth by "casting the bones of their mother over their shoulders," according to Roman poet Ovid (43 BCE–17 CE) in his *Metamorphoses*.

In another myth, Prometheus creates human beings out of clay. This version may explain his close relationship with mortals and his willingness to defy Zeus on their behalf. It also explains why Zeus chooses to punish mortals for Prometheus's transgressions. In all these versions, the name Pandora is somehow connected to the family of Prometheus and to the creation of man. As the first woman, Hesiod's Pandora is a creator of the female half of humankind.

Swiss painter Paul Klee (1879–1940) represented Pandora's box in a 1920 drawing, turning it into a threatening-looking urn suggestive of the female body. German filmmaker G. W. Pabst's (1885–1967) *Pandora's Box* (1929) examined the myth in the context of contemporary society, and featured American actress Louise Brooks (1906–1985) as a tragic femme fatale. German painter Max Beckman (1884–1950) revised an earlier painting after World War II (1939–1945) to equate the contents of Pandora's box with the evils of the atomic bomb. People continue to use the phrase *Pandora's box* today to refer to the unwelcome and unintended consequences of ill-conceived human actions.

DEBORAH LYONS

Bibliography

Hesiod, and M. L. West, trans. *Theogony; and Works and Days*. New York: Oxford University Press, 1999.

Homer, and Robert Fagles, trans. *The Iliad*. New York: Penguin USA, 2003.

Pausanias, and Peter Levi, trans. *Guide to Greece*. New York: Viking Press, 1984.

SEE ALSO: Athena; Deucalion; Flood Myths; Gaia; Graces; Helen; Hephaestus; Hermes; Paris; Prometheus; Zeus.

PARIS

In Greek mythology Paris was a handsome Trojan prince who eloped with Helen, wife of Menelaus, king of Sparta, and later married her. He is often blamed for causing the Trojan War and instigating the fall of the great Phrygian city of Troy.

Above: In this illustration by British illustrator H. J. Ford (1860–1941), Paris begs forgiveness from his former wife, Oenone. The Trojan prince left the nymph, who had magical healing powers, for Helen, wife of the king of Sparta. He returned to seek treatment for a fatal wound he received during the Trojan War.

While Paris was still in the womb, his mother, Hecuba, queen of Troy and wife of Priam, dreamed that she gave birth to a firebrand. Paris's sister, the seer Cassandra, told her parents that the child about to be born would bring ruin upon the city and that he would be a firebrand of destruction for Troy. Although Cassandra had been cursed by Apollo so that no one ever believed her predictions, Priam decided to avoid any danger his son might pose to the Trojans. He gave the baby to a servant to take him far away from Troy. The servant left the child on Mount Ida. Abandoning unwanted children to die in the wilderness or be found for adoption, known as exposure, was an accepted Greek practice, and not uncommon.

Like Oedipus in ancient Greek mythology and Moses in the Old Testament, Paris did not die in the wilderness. He was found by a shepherd who raised him and taught him to be a shepherd himself. On Mount Ida Paris grew up to become an attractive young man and eventually married the nymph Oenone. The couple lived a peaceful rural existence until several of Priam's servants seized one of Paris's favorite bulls. The bull would serve as a prize in funeral games that were being held at Troy (some versions of the myth state that these games were being held in honor of Priam and Hecuba's lost son, Paris). Paris went to Troy to reclaim his bull. According to different versions of the myth, when Paris won all the contests at these games, he was recognized by either Cassandra or Hecuba. The king and queen welcomed back their son, putting aside the firebrand dream and Cassandra's prophecy.

The Judgment of Paris

Before Paris went to Troy to retrieve his bull, the goddesses Hera, Athena, and Aphrodite had visited him while he was watching his flocks on Mount Ida. They came to settle the challenge Eris had issued at the wedding of Peleus, son of Aeacus, king of Aegina, and the Nereid Thetis. Eris, goddess of discord, had not been invited to the event, so she appeared at the wedding to create disharmony among the guests. Into the midst of the wedding guests she rolled a golden apple inscribed with a single line: "To the Fairest." Three of the guests—Hera, Athena, and Aphrodite—all claimed the apple but could not agree to whom it should belong. Neither Zeus nor any other immortal wanted to judge which of these three powerful deities was the fairest. Eventually Zeus instructed Hermes, messenger of the gods, to descend to the earth and appoint a mortal judge. Hermes selected Paris to make this difficult decision.

Each of the goddesses appeared before Paris and offered him a gift to win his favor. Hera offered him rule over all men, Athena offered wisdom and victory in battle, and

Aphrodite offered him the most beautiful woman in the world as his wife. One version of the myth recounts that Aphrodite also offered Paris the quality of powerful sexual attraction. Paris chose Aphrodite, either for her beauty or for the gift she had to offer.

Helen of Troy

The most beautiful woman in ancient Greece was reputed to be Helen, daughter of Zeus and Leda, and wife of Menelaus, king of Sparta. Despite warnings from Cassandra and other seers of Troy—and the objections of his wife, Oenone—Paris set sail for Sparta to claim the prize Aphrodite had promised him. Menelaus and Helen welcomed Paris as a guest in their home and entertained him for nine days. During Paris's stay Menelaus was called to Crete to bury his grandfather, leaving his wife with their guest. This was the opportunity Paris had been waiting for. Before Menelaus returned home, Paris abducted Helen from Sparta.

The couple became lovers on the island of Kranai, off the coast of Greece, then returned to Troy. One version of the myth claims that their journey lasted many weeks while they visited other cities; another reports that they reached Troy in three days. Upon their arrival, the city

Below: The Judgment of Paris *by Italian artist Sandro Botticelli (1445–1510). Despite the offers of gifts made to him by the goddesses Hera and Athena, the Trojan prince hands the golden apple of Eris to Aphrodite, goddess of love. Hera and Athena look on.*

> ## Helen in Egypt
>
> Scholars speculate that Helen might not have gone to Troy at any point. One sixth-century-BCE version of the myth suggests that it was only a cloud image that Paris took to Troy. The real Helen was wafted by the gods to Egypt, where she stayed, safe and pure, hoping that someday she would be able to return to Sparta and her beloved husband. Euripides' *Helen* gives the most complete account of this version. The playwright develops the character of the world's most beautiful woman; meanwhile the play allowed Euripides to speak out against the war that Athens was waging against Sparta at the time.

celebrated their marriage. The Trojans welcomed the prince and his new wife into the city, even though some members of Paris's family had reservations. Cassandra maintained that the marriage was fated to bring ruin to the city of Troy. However, because of Apollo's curse, her protestations were ignored.

Accounts of Helen's departure from Sparta differ: some say she was abducted against her will, others say that she was spellbound by Paris and followed him. Whether Helen went willingly or not, Paris was guilty of violating one of the most fundamental laws of Greek society: the law of *xenia* (hospitality). Ancient Greeks believed that the bond between host and guest was sacred and was governed by Zeus himself. Anyone who failed to abide by *xenia* was sure to suffer terrible consequences.

Above: In this 18th-century painting, Italian artist Giovanni Scaiaro depicts Paris forcefully loading Helen, wife of Menelaus, the king of Sparta, onto a boat destined for Troy. In some versions of the myth Helen is abducted by Paris; in others she accompanies Paris willingly.

Meanwhile Menelaus returned to Sparta and flew into a rage at discovering what had happened to his wife. He and his brother Agamemnon, king of Mycenae, determined to bring Helen back to Sparta and gathered an army of Greek soldiers for this purpose. Some of these soldiers had been Helen's suitors before she married Menelaus and were bound by an oath they had taken swearing to attack any person who endangered Menelaus's marriage to Helen. The bond had been engineered by the hero Odysseus many years earlier.

Following Helen's departure from Sparta, the Greek fleet set sail from Aulis to Troy. The army had been delayed at Aulis until King Agamemnon appeased the anger of Artemis, goddess of the hunt. She demanded that he sacrifice his firstborn daughter, Iphigeneia, before she would send a wind to carry the fleet to Troy. Iphigeneia's death instilled in Agamemnon a desire to bring a special vengeance upon the Trojans and their prince.

The Trojan War

During the course of the Trojan War, which lasted 10 years, Paris's courage was tested by Hector, his brother. Before the conflict Hector, leader of the Trojan forces, accused Paris of being deceitful, obsessed with women, and a coward. He taunted Paris and urged him to stand against Menelaus. He argued that this would be a contest in which the good looks of the wife-stealer would be of little use. Eventually Paris confronted Menelaus to prove how unfair Hector's accusations had been. However, the contest was not a straightforward duel: when Menelaus was about to capture Paris, Aphrodite intervened and spirited him from the battlefield. Paris did not stay away from the conflict for long, however. In his epic the *Iliad,* Homer (c. ninth–eighth century BCE) describes how Paris returned to the fray later. He draws comparisons between Paris running to the battlefield and a horse galloping free across a plain. Hector witnessed this enthusiasm for war and praised his brother.

Although it was clear to some Trojans that Paris was responsible for inciting the war, he did not feel responsible. On occasion he justified his role in events leading up to the conflict. He asserted to Hector that a man is obliged to accept any gifts the gods give; Paris was adamant that he had no choice but to pursue Helen and that she could not resist following him (in *The Trojan Women* by Euripides [c. 486–c. 406 BCE], Helen justified to Hecuba her departure from Sparta with the same explanation). Late in the war Helen rued her captivity in Troy and related to her husband her anguish at being surrounded by devastation, but throughout the conflict her attraction to Paris did not falter.

Although Paris was derided by Hector at times, he played a major role in the long war by avenging the death of his brother and killing Achilles, champion of the Achaeans. Before Hector died he warned Achilles that he would die at Paris's hands. One version of the Achilles myth reports that the Greek hero had a vulnerable heel, the one place not protected by the magical powers of the Styx River into which his mother Thetis had dipped him as a child. Assisted by the god Apollo, Paris managed to fire an arrow that struck mighty Achilles at this vulnerable point, killing him.

Below: In the foreground of this painting by German artist Matthias Gerung (c. 1500–1568/1570), Paris judges which of the three goddesses, Athena, Hera, or Aphrodite, is the most attractive. The Trojan War rages behind them.

Although Aphrodite protected Paris throughout the war, the Trojan prince did not survive the fall of Troy. Once the Trojan horse had been brought into the city and the Greeks rushed through the streets, Paris was hunted down to his father's palace. One of Helen's previous suitors, Philoctetes, who fought with the bow of Heracles, shot an arrow that mortally wounded Paris.

As Paris lay on his deathbed, he remembered his first wife, Oenone, who had the power to heal any wound from which he might suffer. He asked to be taken to her on Mount Ida. Oenone was still angry about being replaced by Helen, however. She refused to help Paris and sent him back to Troy. Later she felt remorseful and rushed to Troy to save him, but she was too late: Paris had died from the wound inflicted by Philoctetes. He did not live to witness the slaughter of his fellow Trojans or to see the walls of Troy catch fire and the great Phrygian city collapse.

Paris in art

Of all the ancient Greek legends, the Judgment of Paris was one of the most popular in postclassical art. Artists favored the scene because of its aesthetic appeal. Many artists have used this part of the myth to reflect contemporary culture. German painter Lucas Cranach

Above: In this painting by Italian artist Giovanni Domenico Tiepolo (1727–1804), Trojans heave the wooden horse through the streets of Troy. The horse concealed enemy soldiers.

(1472–1553), for example, depicted Paris as a knight in armor and Hermes as a faithful attendant at his side, wearing a winged hat and holding his caduceus (a wing-topped staff entwined with two serpents). The three goddesses are naked except for necklaces that match their German-style coiffures. It is not clear which deity is Athena or Hera, but Aphrodite can be identified as the figure pointing to the sky where Eros, the god of sexual love, aims his bow at her.

Flemish painter Peter Paul Rubens (1577–1640) often represented the female figure nude. In his *Judgment of Paris*, the hero is depicted as a shepherd and Hermes stands behind him. While the figures of the goddesses are similar to each other in appearance, a peacock, the sacred bird of Hera, struts near her and a shield rests behind Athena. In his version, Rubens suggests the final destructive outcome of Paris's judgment by placing a Fury (a deity of retribution) in the sky above the scene.

American artist Bob Thompson (1937–1966) represented the scene more recently. In his version the goddesses are painted in vibrant colors, and the characters appear in an exotic setting, far removed from the carefully constructed landscapes painted by Rubens

and Cranach. The myth also appealed to the Spanish surrealist painter Salvador Dalí (1904–1989), whose 1965 lithograph depicts the naked Hera, Athena, and Aphrodite towering above a small and confused Paris. In stark contrast to the ancient vase paintings in which the Judgment of Paris was first recorded is American painter Charles Bell's (1935–1995) rendition of the event. In 1986 Bell arranged a number of Barbie dolls to reflect Cranach's *Judgment of Paris* and painted the scene. Female dolls represented Hera, Athena, and Aphrodite, while male dolls represented Hermes and Paris. Although the myth of Paris has its roots in ancient Greece, the Judgment of Paris remains a source of inspiration for artists today.

KARELISA HARTIGAN

Bibliography

Bulfinch, Thomas. *Bulfinch's Mythology*. New York: Modern Library, 1998.

Euripides, and Paul Roche, trans. *10 Plays*. New York: Signet Classics, 1998.

Graves, Robert. *The Greek Myths*. New York: Penguin USA, 1993.

Homer, and Robert Fagles, trans. *The Iliad*. New York: Penguin USA, 2003.

SEE ALSO: Achilles; Agamemnon; Aphrodite; Apollo; Athena; Cassandra; Hector; Hecuba; Helen; Hera; Heracles; Hermes; Menelaus; Odysseus; Philoctetes; Priam; Zeus.

PASIPHAE

Pasiphae was a daughter of Helios, the Greek sun god. Her mother, Perse, was the daughter of the Titans Oceanus and Tethys, who were parents of numerous marine divinities. In addition to Pasiphae, the children of Perse and Helios included Circe, Aeetes, and Perses.

Like her sister Circe and her niece Medea, Pasiphae possessed powers of sorcery. She was married to Minos, the king of the island of Crete, and is famous for giving birth to the monstrous Minotaur, the product of an unnatural love affair with a white bull. It was her husband's offense against Poseidon that brought tragedy upon unsuspecting Pasiphae, and her myth illustrated that innocence was no protection from harm.

After defeating his brothers to claim the throne of Crete, Minos still had many challengers and sought to cement his authority. He declared that the gods would validate his right to rule by granting him whatever he prayed for. Minos asked his uncle Poseidon, god of the sea, to send him a bull, which he would then sacrifice to the god. A beautiful snow white bull emerged from the sea, guaranteeing Minos's succession to the throne.

Minos, however, considered the creature too beautiful to sacrifice, so he put it to pasture and killed another in its place. This breach of a promise incurred Poseidon's wrath. The god made Pasiphae, not Minos, the direct victim of his revenge, however, and caused her to fall in love with the bull. This act ensured that Minos, to his eternal shame, would be forever remembered less as a king than as a husband whose wife had cheated on him with a bull. Unlike other cultures that embraced animal gods, in Greek mythology, animals ranked far below gods and humans. Sexual relations with animals brought shame and dishonor.

According to another, very different version, however, Pasiphae herself neglected to offer due sacrifices to Aphrodite. The goddess was so angry that she punished Pasiphae by making her fall in love with the bull.

Driven mad by her unspeakable passion for the bull, Pasiphae finally sought the assistance of Daedalus, the master architect and inventor in the palace. At the queen's request he built a hollow wooden cow and covered it with cowhide. He made the sham cow so craftily that it could be mistaken for the real thing. Pasiphae hid inside the cow, and when it was wheeled to the bull's pasture, the bull copulated with it and at last satisfied Pasiphae's desire.

Later, to her horror, Pasiphae gave birth to a creature with a bull's head and tail and a man's body. It was named Asterius but was usually called the Minotaur ("bull of Minos"), for it was an enduring reminder of Minos's folly.

Like all hybrid creatures in Greek mythology, the Minotaur's monstrous appearance was matched by its violent nature. The horrified Minos asked Daedalus to build an asylum for the man-beast. So Daedalus designed the Labyrinth, a vast underground maze of a palace that kept the Minotaur confined. The Labyrinth was so cleverly constructed that anyone going in would never find his way out again.

Right: In Greek mythology gods often changed shape to seduce mortals. In this Greek mosaic, Phoenician princess Europa is abducted by the god Zeus, who has changed shape to become a bull.

Below: This 16th-century painting by an anonymous artist often referred to as Master of the Cassoni Campana (fl. c. 1510) depicts Pasiphae setting off to visit the white bull with whom she is having an affair.

Gods, Women, and Animals

Women having amorous relationships with animals is a recurring feature of Greek mythology. In most instances the animal in question was actually a god using a disguise to seduce the woman. If gods took on animal forms, they could always regain their divine shapes. For instance, Poseidon appeared as a bird to Medusa, as a bull to Canace, as a dolphin to Melantho, as a horse to Demeter, and as a ram to Theophane. Zeus's bestial forms included appearing as a swan to Leda and as a bull to Europa, who bore him Minos.

Seduced women were also transformed by gods into animals: Zeus made Io into a cow and Callisto into a bear, and Poseidon made Theophane into a ewe. Women's transformations into animals or other forms, such as trees or streams, were usually permanent. There are no examples of goddesses in animal form seducing men. Scholars speculate that various principles held by ancient Greeks could explain why in mythology women were seduced by animals. In the patriarchal ancient Greek society virginity and chastity in women were highly valued qualities. One theory claims that animal disguises adopted by the gods symbolically overcame any resistance that a woman made to protect her sexual purity. Scholars also attribute the permanence of most transformations of women to this high regard for the preservation of sexual purity.

Ocean Monsters

It is no coincidence that Pasiphae and her sorcering relatives are all related to ocean divinities. The ocean was a mysterious place in Greek myth. It had unseen depths and could change unpredictably. Not only did most monsters have their origins in the deep, but many of them were female. Some scholars have argued that these female characters reflected attitudes toward women held by male storytellers—who may have regarded women as mysterious and unknowable, like the sea.

These ocean-bred female monstrosities include Scylla, Charybdis, the Gorgons, the Harpies, Chimaera, the Sphinx, Ceto, the Graeae, and Echidna. Scylla, Charybdis, and Echidna preyed upon sailors. The Gorgons petrified men with their gaze. The Harpies, the hounds of Zeus, plagued Phineas (a blind seer-king) and harassed the hero Aeneas and his men. The Sphinx terrorized young Theban men, and Chimaera ravaged the Lycian countryside (a region in western Asia). All these monsters were given to sudden attack and could be overcome only by cunning.

Pasiphae and her relatives were not monsters, but they possessed extraordinary powers that disrupted the natural world. Pasiphae put an end to Minos's sex life by making him ejaculate snakes and scorpions. Her sister, Circe, unmanned her male visitors by transforming them into sentient animals. Medea, Aeetes' daughter and Pasiphae's niece, helped Jason, the hero who went on a quest for the Golden Fleece. She put to sleep a sleepless dragon, rejuvenated a ram, and slew her own brother, her children, and the family of Jason's intended Greek bride. Despite their charms, these ocean offspring could never have successful relationships with mortal men.

Left: Flemish artist Bartholomaeus Spranger (1546–1611) depicts an encounter between Glaucus and the water nymph Scylla. Scylla was later turned into a fearsome sea monster.

Pasiphae and Minos's children

Pasiphae bore Minos many children: Androgeos, Catreus, Deucalion, Glaucus, Acacallis, Xenodice, Ariadne, and Phaedra. Most of them lived unfortunate lives and suffered violent and premature deaths. Androgeos grew up in Athens and met an early death, either fighting the Marathonian Bull—the same bull that Pasiphae had desired—or by ambush. Blaming King Aegeus of Athens for his son's demise, Minos demanded that every nine years Athens send a tribute of seven young men and seven young women to be sacrificial victims for the Minotaur.

This practice continued until Athenian hero Theseus killed the Minotaur. Theseus succeeded where others had failed because he seduced Ariadne, who secured him Daedalus's assistance in entering and leaving the Labyrinth. Their love did not last. After eloping with her, Theseus abandoned her on the island of Naxos. Ariadne either took her own life or married the god Dionysus.

Phaedra, who did marry Theseus, also died by her own hand out of shame. According to one version, Aphrodite made her fall in love with her stepson, Hippolytus, and the boy rejected her advances.

The curse of Pasiphae

Like his philandering father Zeus, king of the gods, Minos repeatedly cheated on his wife. According to Greek scholar and historian Apollodorus (fl. 140 BCE), Pasiphae was furious with Minos for his affairs, and she showed herself much more adept than Zeus's wife, Hera, at punishing both her husband and his mistresses. She shrewdly resorted to her powers of sorcery and put a curse on Minos so that whenever he had sex with another woman, he ejaculated scorpions and snakes. This put a damper on his sexual escapades, for all his lovers perished.

However, in spite of his affliction, Minos was able to have an affair with Procris, who sought refuge on Crete after her husband, Cephalus, had discovered her infidelity with a man named Pteleon. According to Apollodorus, Minos wanted to make Procris his mistress, but she declined because she perceived that he had been enchanted. Once Procris found out about Minos's sexual

Left: This bust is an anonymous sculptor's impression of the Minotaur. In Greek mythology this fearsome monster has a human body and a bull's head and tail.

problems, however, she gave him a healing potion that enabled her to sleep with him without coming to any harm. In the racier account by Greek mythographer Antoninus Liberalis (second century CE), Procris made a condom of sorts out of a goat bladder. Minos would have sex and ejaculate the dangerous creatures into the condom.

In gratitude, Minos awarded Procris with a javelin that never missed its target and his hound Laelaps, who always caught whatever it chased. Procris then returned home, where she was reunited with her husband. The pair went hunting—making use of the gifts acquired from Minos—only for Procris to die when Cephalus threw the infallible javelin at her by mistake.

Pasiphae's curse, meanwhile, had ultimately backfired, since it was overcome by the very thing she had meant to deny her husband—another adulterous affair.

Depictions of Pasiphae

According to Greek travel writer Pausanias (143–176 CE), there were bronze statues of Pasiphae and Helios in the sanctuary of Ino at Thalamae in Laconia (a region in Greece). There, Pasiphae, which means "all-shining," was a title of the moon goddess Selene. Ino, escaping her husband Athamas's murderous rage by jumping into the ocean, had been transformed into the sea deity Leucothea. This "white goddess" helped sailors at sea, hence her association with other divinities who provided means of navigation, such as the sun (Helios) and the moon (Pasiphae).

A first-century-CE wall painting in the House of the Vettii in Pompeii, Italy, depicts Daedalus, Pasiphae, and the wooden cow. French painter Henri Matisse (1869–1954) made two graphic prints: *Pasiphae* and *Pasiphae Hugging an Olive Tree*. American artist Jackson Pollock (1912–1956) also represented Pasiphae in a painting called *Pasiphae*.

KATHRYN CHEW

Bibliography

Apollodorus, and Robin Hard, trans. *The Library of Greek Mythology*. New York: Oxford University Press, 1999.
Howatson, M. C., and Ian Chilvers. *Concise Oxford Companion to Classical Literature*. New York: Oxford University Press, 1993.
Pausanias, and Peter Levi, trans. *Guide to Greece*. New York: Viking Press, 1984.

SEE ALSO: Ariadne; Circe; Crete; Daedalus; Hippolytus; Minos; Poseidon; Theseus; Zeus.

PATROCLUS

Patroclus is famous for his loyal friendship to the great Greek hero Achilles, and for his tragic death on the battlefield during the Trojan War.

According to legend, Patroclus was the son of Menoetius, one of the Argonauts. Patroclus was one of the many suitors who hoped to marry Helen, the most beautiful woman in the world. Her stepfather Tyndareos feared that the suitors who failed to win her hand might be resentful, so, at Odysseus's suggestion, he made them all swear to support whichever of them Helen chose, and to fight anyone who tried to harm the marriage. Eventually Helen chose a Greek prince named Menelaus. When Paris, son of the Trojan king Priam, later ran away with her, the Greeks, including Helen's suitors, went to attack Troy. So began the Trojan War.

Below: The slave girl Briseis is being passed to Agamemnon (seated) in this Roman painting from the first century CE. The figure between them is usually identified as Achilles.

By this time, Patroclus had another reason for going to Troy. He had killed a young man, Clitonymus, in a quarrel. He went into hiding in the house of Peleus, king of Phthia. There he struck up a close friendship with Achilles, the son of Peleus and the goddess Thetis. When the Trojan War began, Patroclus went to Troy to support Achilles, who was one of the Greeks' best fighters.

A sensible friend

Although Achilles was the higher born and better fighter of the two friends, Patroclus was older. Before they left, Peleus asked Patroclus to look after Achilles and to give him guidance and advice. Patroclus was perfectly suited to this task. He was kind, caring, and sensible, qualities that set him apart from the hotheaded and petulant Achilles. However, Achilles' childishness still caused trouble. In the 10th year of the war, he argued with Agamemnon, king of Mycenae and leader of the Greek forces, over a slave girl named Briseis, who lived with Achilles in his camp. This argument set in motion a chain of events that eventually led to Patroclus's death.

Agamemnon had been forced to give up his own slave girl, Chryseis, by the god Apollo. Angry at this loss, he decided to replace her with Briseis and sent his men to

Achilles' tent to fetch her. Patroclus had no choice but to hand her over to Agamemnon's men. The seizure of Briseis left Achilles furious. He was so angry that he refused to fight, or to let his men fight, for the Greek side. This was disastrous, because Achilles was a great soldier. With him off the battlefield, the Trojans soon gained the upper hand.

Nestor's plan

Achilles' petulance filled Patroclus with shame. Nestor, one of the oldest and wisest of the Greek leaders, suggested that if he could not persuade Achilles to change his mind, Patroclus might consider going into battle himself, disguised as Achilles, to scare the Trojans away. Patroclus agreed to go along with Nestor's plan.

By the time that Patroclus visited Achilles to implore him to fight, the Trojans had driven the Greeks so far back toward the sea that there was a danger they might set fire to the Greek ships. Achilles still refused to join in the battle himself. However, the danger was so great that he agreed to let Patroclus ride into battle disguised as him, but he told his friend that he must only chase the Trojans away from the ships, and then retreat. Patroclus put on Achilles' armor and led his men into battle. The ploy was a huge success. Many Trojans were killed, and the Trojan forces were forced back toward the walls of their city.

However, Patroclus did not heed Achilles' advice. Carried away with his success, Patroclus did not retreat, as Achilles had asked him to, but followed the Trojans across the battlefield. The god Apollo, who supported the Trojans in the war, knocked off Patroclus's helmet and tore his breastplate from his body, leaving him extremely vulnerable and revealing to the Trojans that it was not Achilles fighting but an imposter. First the Trojan Euphorbus struck him with a spear, weakening him considerably. Then Hector, the leader of the Trojan forces, killed him.

The horrified Greeks collected the body of Patroclus from the battlefield and took it to Achilles' camp. Achilles was overcome with grief. Desperate to avenge his dear friend's death, he returned to the battlefield and fought Hector in single combat, eventually killing him. Achilles' anger was still so great that for the next 12 days he drove his chariot around the walls of Troy, dragging Hector's body behind him. Later, when Achilles himself was killed by Paris, his ashes were mingled with those of Patroclus and placed in a golden urn made by Hephaestus, blacksmith of the gods. In this way, the two friends were united for eternity.

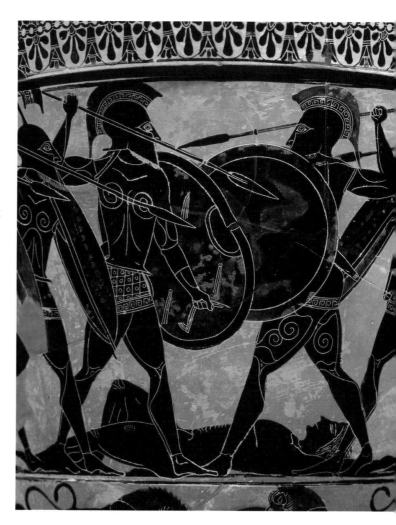

Above: This illustration from a sixth-century-BCE wine jar shows Greek and Trojan warriors fighting over the body of Patroclus.

Sources for Patroclus's story

The main source for the story of Patroclus is the *Iliad*, an epic poem about the last year of the Trojan War composed by Greek poet Homer (c. ninth–eighth century BCE). Many other ancient writers also referred to Patroclus. Among them were Apollodorus (third century BCE) and Pindar (c. 522–c. 438 BCE).

Although he was not the most famous of the heroes of the Trojan War, Patroclus played a central role in its story: his actions served as the catalyst that led to the deaths of Achilles and Hector. He also embodied many noble qualities, including courage, loyalty, and humility.

ANNA CLAYBOURNE

Bibliography

Homer, and Robert Fagles, trans. *The Iliad*. New York: Penguin USA, 2003.

SEE ALSO: Achilles; Agamemnon; Apollo; Hector; Helen; Menelaus; Nestor; Paris; Peleus; Priam.

PELEUS

Peleus, a hero of ancient Greek myth, was the son of Aeacus, mythical king of Aegina, a Greek island southwest of Athens. His mother was Endeis. His siblings included his half brothers Telamon (father of the Trojan War hero Ajax) and Phocos. The distinguished hero Achilles was the son of Peleus and the sea goddess Thetis.

Aeacus banished Peleus and Telamon from Aegina after they had joined forces to kill their half brother Phocos. Peleus proceeded to Phthia in northern Greece, where he entered the service of a king in order to be "purified" for taking human life outside battle. Eurytion, king of Phthia, performed the purification, and Peleus married his daughter Antigone (not to be confused with Oedipus's daughter of the same name).

Peleus and Eurytion then went to the city of Calydon in Aetolia (a region in Greece) in order to aid some heroes who were seeking to rid the land of a ravenous wild boar. The boar had been sent by the goddess Artemis, who was angry at Oeneus, the local king, for omitting her in offerings to the gods. During the Calydonian boar hunt Peleus killed Eurytion with a miscast spear, was again driven into exile, and again sought purification. The killing may have been intentional—with his father-in-law out of the way, Peleus himself would have been able to gain control of Phthia.

The treachery of Astydameia

This time Peleus was purified by Acastus, king of the city of Iolcus in Thessaly in northeast Greece. Afterward Peleus competed in funeral games for Pelias, Acastus's father and predecessor, during which he wrestled the female warrior Atalanta, another veteran of the Calydonian boar hunt. Later, however, Acastus's wife, Astydameia, tried to seduce Peleus. When he resisted, she sent word to Antigone that he was going to marry her own daughter Sterope. Antigone, believing herself abandoned, committed suicide.

Astydameia then told Acastus that she had been raped by Peleus. Although desiring revenge, the king could not harm the man he had purified without violating religious law. So he took Peleus hunting on nearby Mount Pelion, stole his sword, and abandoned him while he slept, so that Peleus would become prey for centaurs, vicious half-man, half-horse creatures that inhabited the area. Peleus managed to save himself after being given a sword by the wise centaur Cheiron. In another version the gods gave him a sword.

Later Peleus gathered a force of soldiers, including the heroes Castor, Pollux, and Jason. With them he stormed Iolcus and killed Astydameia and, according to Greek scholar and historian Apollodorus (fl. 140 BCE), also Acastus.

Left: The Calydonian boar hunt is depicted in this second-century-BCE alabaster relief.

Right: In this painting Italian artist Pompeo Girolamo Batoni (1708–1787) depicts the centaur Cheiron teaching Achilles to play the lyre.

After other adventures, including service as an Argonaut, Peleus married Polydora, who was a Spartan princess. In another version Polydora was Peleus's daughter rather than his wife. Later Peleus married the sea goddess Thetis. She was the daughter of the sea god Nereus and was courted by the gods Zeus and Poseidon. It was revealed that her son would be more powerful than his father, however, so Zeus resolved to marry Thetis to a mortal in order to prevent the birth of a son who could challenge him.

The Judgment of Paris

Thetis had the power to change shape, so Peleus enlisted the help of the centaur Cheiron to capture her and make her his wife. The marriage, celebrated on Mount Pelion, was attended by all the gods except the goddess Eris (meaning "strife"), who was not invited. To cause trouble, she tossed a golden apple inscribed "To the Fairest" among the guests. Three goddesses, Hera, Athena, and Aphrodite, claimed the apple. Zeus arranged for Paris, son of the king of Troy, to judge.

Paris decided for Aphrodite, who promised him the most beautiful woman in the world. That woman was Helen, wife of Menelaus, king of Sparta in Greece. With Aphrodite's help, Paris took Helen to Troy, causing the Greeks to attack Troy and thus setting off the Trojan War. Through one of the distortions in chronology that occasionally occur in Greek mythology, the only son of Peleus and Thetis, Achilles, was old enough to fight at Troy, where Paris killed him.

Achilles and Cheiron

Thetis had hoped to immortalize Achilles and, as an infant, placed him in the hearth fire at night in order to burn away his mortal part. Peleus observed this and accused her of trying to kill their son. Thetis, enraged at Peleus's lack of faith, left and returned to the sea. Unable to raise Achilles alone, Peleus took him to Cheiron, who raised and instructed him in warfare. In the *Iliad*, an epic poem by Homer (c. ninth–eighth century BCE), Peleus was accompanied on this mission by two exiles then living at his court in Phthia, Phoenix and Patroclus. Patroclus remained with Achilles and Cheiron, while Peleus installed Phoenix as king of the Dolopians, a people who lived in Thessaly.

Peleus was elderly by the time the war broke out, and he stayed in Phthia. Taking advantage of the absence of most Greek warriors, the sons of Acastus attacked Phthia and drove Peleus from power; soon after, according to the version by Apollodorus, he died in exile. According to another version, Achilles' son Neoptolemus, together with Thetis, intervened to save Peleus.

Many scenes from Peleus's life featured on ancient Greek vase paintings. The wedding of Peleus and Thetis is the main scene depicted on the François Vase (c. 570 BCE) by artist Kleitias, and Peleus is also pictured at the Calydonian boar hunt. Other scenes on black-figure amphorae (two-handled urns) include Peleus wrestling Atalanta and chasing Thetis.

JIM MARKS

Bibliography

Homer, and Robert Fagles, trans. *The Iliad*. New York: Penguin USA, 2003.
Howatson, M. C., and Ian Chilvers. *Concise Oxford Companion to Classical Literature*. New York: Oxford University Press, 1993.

SEE ALSO: Achilles; Atalanta; Castor and Pollux; Helen; Jason; Paris; Patroclus; Thetis.

PELOPS

Pelops, a Greek hero, was the son of Tantalus, king of Argos (or in some versions king of Corinth or of Lydia). Pelops won a famous chariot race with the king Oenomaus to gain the hand in marriage of the king's beautiful daughter, Hippodameia.

Above: Pelops is depicted sitting on a throne in this marble relief, which adorns a Roman sarcophagus found in North Africa. His wife, Hippodameia, stands next to him.

When Tantalus invited the gods to a feast, they were glad to accept. Tantalus was said to be a son of Zeus, the king of the gods, and had often shared the gods' hospitality on Mount Olympus. The main course at the feast was a meat stew, well spiced and savory, but the gods felt that something about it was not quite right. Only the goddess Demeter, who was mourning the kidnap of her daughter Persephone by Hades, the god of the underworld, ate some of the stew. While she distractedly nibbled at a bone, the other gods demanded to know what the stew was made of. Tantalus laughed and told the gods that it was his own son, Pelops.

Tantalus had wanted to see whether the gods would realize that the stew contained human flesh, but the gods were disgusted at Tantalus's impiety. They brought Pelops back to life by boiling his bones in a magic cauldron, and Demeter gave him an ivory shoulder blade to replace the bone that she had chewed. Pelops emerged from the cauldron twice as handsome as he had been before.

The gods curse Tantalus

The gods became even more outraged with Tantalus when they later discovered that he had also stolen nectar and ambrosia from their own feasts to share with his human friends. They destroyed Tantalus's kingdom, and when he died and went to the underworld, they devised a special punishment for him.

Tantalus was suspended from the branches of a fruit tree laden with all kinds of luscious fruit, over the waters of a muddy lake. When he leaned down to drink, the waters of the lake retreated, so that he could never quench his thirst. When he tried to pluck some fruit to satisfy his hunger, the wind blew the branches out of his reach. In this way he was condemned to eternal thirst and hunger. The word *tantalize*, derived from his name, reminds us of his fate.

Meanwhile, Pelops and his followers gathered up the treasures of the realm and set out to found a new kingdom. One of the places they visited was Elis (a region in southern Greece), where Oenomaus was king.

Oenomaus had a beautiful daughter named Hippodameia. He guarded her very closely indeed because an oracle had told him that the man whom Hippodameia married would cause his death. Oenomaus challenged any

Right: This coastline forms part of the the Peloponnese. It is named after the ancient Greek hero Pelops and marks the territory he once controlled.

suitor who asked for his daughter's hand to a chariot race, after which the winner would be allowed to kill the loser. The stakes were so high because Oenomaus knew that he was nearly impossible to beat. The horses that were harnessed to his chariot had been given to him by his father, Ares, god of war, and could run faster even than the north wind. His charioteer, Myrtilus, was a son of Hermes, the speedy messenger god, and was famous throughout Greece for his driving skills.

In spite of the heavy odds against them, however, suitors continued to present themselves because Hippodameia was very beautiful and the kingdom of Elis was very rich. One by one, each of them lost the race, after which Oenomaus killed him and nailed his head to the palace gates.

The chariot race

Pelops was not deterred by the rows of heads facing him as he approached the palace. Poseidon, god of the sea, had given him a fast golden chariot that was able to race across water. When Hippodameia saw Pelops, she fell in love with him immediately.

She feared that he also would suffer the fate of the other suitors and decided to do her best to help him. Together with Pelops, she bribed her father's charioteer, Myrtilus, to sabotage Oenomaus's chariot by replacing the pins that held the wheels on the chariot's axles with wax plugs. Myrtilus's reward was to be half of the kingdom.

The race began. Oenomaus knew that Pelops would be harder to beat than the other suitors. He let Pelops get slightly ahead, and then he stood up and poised his spear to fling at Pelops to kill him. At that moment the wax pins melted completely, and Oenomaus's chariot crashed and killed him.

Pelops had won the race and the hand of Hippodameia, but he had no intention of keeping his side of the bargain with Myrtilus. He killed him by throwing him into the sea. Before Myrtilus drowned, however, he managed to curse Pelops and all his descendants.

Pelops and Hippodameia ruled Oenomaus's kingdom and extended it by conquering neighboring regions. Their rule covered a large part of Greece, and the southern peninsula of Greece is still known today as the Peloponnese, which means "Pelops's land."

As for the curse of Myrtilus, it hung over all Pelops's descendants, including his son Atreus, his grandsons Agamemnon and Menelaus, and his great-grandson Orestes.

A shrine to Pelops at Olympia, a city in Elis, was said to have been built by Heracles, one of Pelops's most renowned descendants. Artistic representations of Pelops include a sculpture on the temple of Zeus at Olympia, which shows the moment before the chariot race began. According to Greek travel writer Pausanias (143–176 CE), the race was also depicted on the seventh-century-BCE Chest of Cypselus.

PETER CONNOR

Bibliography

Bulfinch, Thomas. *Bulfinch's Mythology.* New York: Modern Library, 1998.
Howatson, M. C., and Ian Chilvers. *Concise Oxford Companion to Classical Literature.* New York: Oxford University Press, 1993.

SEE ALSO: Agamemnon; Ares; Atreus; Heracles; Hermes; Menelaus; Orestes; Philoctetes; Poseidon.

PENATES

The Penates were among the most important household gods of the ancient Romans, along with Vesta, the Lares, and the genii. Romans recognized two types of Penates, domestic and public. They distinguished between the private worship of the Penates in the home and the public worship of the Penates as protective gods of the state. The domestic Penates were not depicted in a recognizable way, but the public Penates, considered indispensable to the very existence of the city, had a clear visual image.

The name Penates itself helps define the nature of these gods. The Latin word *penates* is based on *penus*, a noun that refers both to food and to the place in which provisions were stored. The *penus* was further defined as the innermost recess of the house, where the essentials of life were safeguarded. This notion that the *penus* was at the very heart of the home is reflected in the related verb *penetrare*, meaning "to penetrate, to get to the interior." The second element of Penates is the suffix *–ates*, which indicates that a person or thing belongs to a particular location.

Protectors of the home

The Penates belonged to the *penus*. They were deities of the innermost recesses, the safest area—the heart or core—of the house. In a larger sense the Penates were considered protectors of the home and of everything in the house that was necessary for the family. The word *penates* is virtually always found in the plural and was, in origin, an adjective modifying an unexpressed noun such as gods. Often the word *penates* is used in a general sense.

Latin orator and writer Cicero (106–43 BCE) used the phrase *patrii penatesque di* ("ancestral gods and Penates") to describe all the family gods. The Penates and gods of the ancestors are, in this quite typical usage, synonymous. In fact, it is often assumed that the wide variety of statuettes found in various family shrines of Pompeii and elsewhere indicates that many gods—Venus, Fortune, Bacchus, and Mercury, among others—were worshiped in particular houses and were considered Penates by the families who displayed their images.

The public Penates

The public Penates were revered as the guardians of the state and its most basic needs. They were worshiped as guarantors of Rome's security. In the public sphere the Penates did have a recognizable form. Greek historian Dionysius of Halicarnassus (first century BCE), who lived in Rome, treats this subject at length. In *Roman Antiquities* he describes a small temple of the Penates on the Velia, a hill near the Roman Forum. The images of the gods, he reports, are there on display for all to see, unmistakably

---

Penates in the House

The household gods, including the Penates, were worshiped in the sacrarium (or *lararium*), a shrine in the wall of the atrium (main room) or the kitchen. This family shrine was sometimes in the form of a niche but was often in the more elaborate shape of a small temple front, with columns and triangular pediment.

On the back wall of the shrine there were frequently paintings of the Lares (guardian spirits of the house) and the genii, along with other divinities venerated in a particular family. Statuettes of the gods were normally placed on the floor of the shrines. Family worship consisted of offerings of wheat, flour, and wine.

Latin poet Horace (65–8 BCE) advised his friend Phidyle that the Penates were satisfied "provided that pure hands touch the altar" with the gift of sacred meal mixed with crackling salt. Roman hero Aeneas, in the epic poem the *Aeneid* by Latin poet Virgil (70–19 BCE), followed the usual Roman custom when he urged his companions to call their Penates and ancestral gods to join them in a dinner.

Above: This picture shows an altar to the Roman Lares, discovered in a house in the Roman town of Pompeii. Lares were domestic gods much like Penates, who protected the home.

identified as the Penates by an inscription. Dionysius writes, "They are two seated youths holding spears," and he relates the images to the twin gods of Samothrace (an island in the Aegean Sea), an identification also made by other ancient scholars. This identification was encouraged by the fact that both the Penates and the Samothracian gods (who were, in turn, sometimes equated with the Greek Castor and Pollux) were called the Great Gods (Magni Dei) and shared some iconographic features.

More important than such ancient speculation is the Roman belief that statuettes of the Penates were carried by the hero Aeneas on his voyage from Troy to Italy after the Trojan War. In his epic poem the *Aeneid*, Roman poet Virgil (70–19 BCE) has Aeneas cry out, soon after reaching Italy, "Hail, O Land given to me by the Fates! Hail, O Penates of Troy! This is our home! This is our country!"

The Trojan Penates, in finding a new home in Italy, assure Aeneas and his companions that Italy is indeed their new land. The Romans saw themselves as descendants of the Trojans and the early Latins, among whom Aeneas and his companions were thought to have settled in Lavinium (present-day Pratica di Mare), a village not far from Rome near the Mediterranean coast. There, special veneration of the Penates continued well into the age of the Roman Empire (31 BCE–476 CE).

There is, however, an indication that the Penates of the Velia had come to Rome not from Lavinium but from the mountain settlement of Alba Longa (see box). Roman lore celebrated this place as the homeland of Romulus and Remus (mythical founders of Rome) before they settled with their companions on the site of the future Rome.

Tradition recalled that the third king of Rome, Tullus Hostilius (c. 672–641 BCE), not only defeated Alba Longa but demolished most of it so that it could not rise again. He did this probably because the old mother city was seen as a threat to the safety or ambitions of early Rome. Ancient writers add that the temple of the Penates on the Velia was near or even on the site of the palace of Tullus Hostilius.

The Penates must have been moved from Alba Longa to the Velia, where Tullus Hostilius lived in Rome. This scenario explains the fact that there was another, and probably earlier, public cult of the Penates at Rome, which belonged to the *Penus Vestae*, the "holy of holies" of the

Below: In this fifth-century-CE picture, Aeneas, founder of Rome, is visited by the Penates of Troy, who appear to him in dream.

hearth goddess Vesta, whose worship was established by the second Roman king, Numa Pompilius (c. 715–673 BCE). Religious custom required that Roman civic officials, the consuls and praetors, accompanied by priests, make a joint sacrifice every year to Vesta and the Penates at Lavinium before entering office.

Alba Longa

The Penates had a special place in the legends of Alba Longa. Ascanius, the son of Aeneas, set out to found a colony of Lavinium at Alba Longa 30 years after the arrival of the Trojans in Italy. The colonists built a temple with an inner sanctuary (the *penus*) for the Penates in their new city, but the images of these gods, which Aeneas had brought from Troy, fled the new Alban sanctuary and returned to their pedestals in the old temple at Lavinium. The colonists brought them back to Alba Longa, but the Penates fled again.

The myth explains why the descendants of Aeneas were compelled to return to Lavinium, as were the Albans (and later the Romans), to worship their ancestral Trojan gods. According to this myth, the Penates venerated at Alba Longa itself must thus have been local Alban, not the old Trojan, gods.

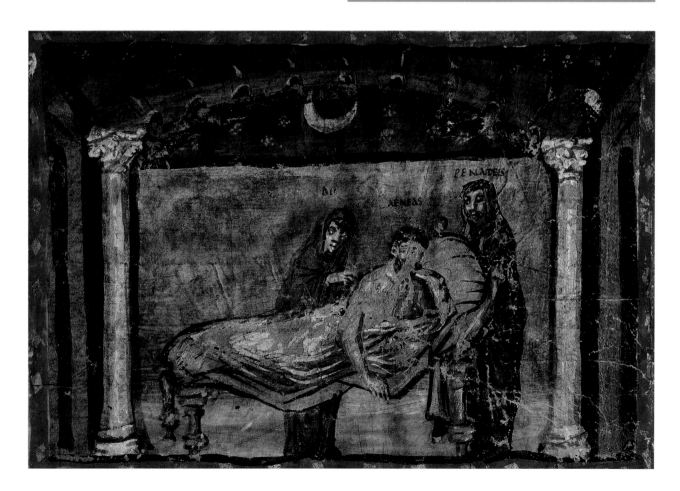

Left: This marble relief is part of the Ara Pacis Augustae, a monument to the Roman emperor Augustus (63 BCE–14 CE). Aeneas is depicted with two children in the sanctuary of the Penates, an area guarded by the spirits.

The importance of the Penates cult is well attested in Lavinium. Greek historian Timaeus (c. 350– 260 BCE) visited the sanctuary and reported that holy objects concerning the Penates were kept there, including iron and bronze heralds' wands and an earthenware vessel from Troy. The wands are reminiscent of the staffs held by the Penates in their Velia temple, and the vessel may well have been an ancient storage jar for food, since it was associated with the Penates.

Archaeological finds

Archaeologists have unearthed a row of 13 archaic altars just below the citadel of Lavinium that date from the sixth to the fourth centuries BCE. They have also found remains of a nearby seventh-century-BCE tomb that was turned into a monument in the fourth century, evidently to serve as the hero shrine of Aeneas.

Not far from the citadel area, near life-size votive statues, along with a fifth-century-BCE statue of the goddess Minerva, have come to light, attesting the presence of a sanctuary for the goddess nearby. The temple of Vesta and of the Penates was probably on the citadel itself.

A relief panel beside the front entry to the Augustan Altar of Peace in Rome depicts Aeneas about to offer a sacrifice. The scene is obviously set in Lavinium. Two youthful figures, surely the Penates, are seated at the front of a little temple and hold staffs. They look down upon Aeneas from the hill above (probably the citadel). The image of these seated figures with their staffs evokes Dionysius's description of the Penates on the Velia in Rome.

By the later fourth century BCE, Lavinium was under the control of the Roman state. Rome maintained religious ties with its Trojan ancestors through annual sacrifices to the Penates of Aeneas's old city, Lavinium. In a similar way, the Romans continued to venerate the Penates of their more immediate mother city, Alba Longa, in the temple on the Velia in Rome. This worship of the Penates was believed essential to assure the continuity and safety of both family and city-state.

DANIEL P. HARMON

Bibliography

Scheid, John, and Janet Lloyd, trans. *An Introduction to Roman Religion*. Bloomington, IN: Indiana University Press, 2003.
Turcan, Robert, and Antonia Nevill, trans. *The Gods of Ancient Rome: Religion in Everyday Life from Archaic to Imperial Times*. New York: Routledge, 2001.

SEE ALSO: Aeneas; Lares; Rome; Vesta.

PENELOPE

Penelope was the wife of the Greek hero Odysseus. Even though her husband took 10 years to return home from the Trojan War, Penelope never gave up hope that he might come back. She thus came to be seen as the epitome of fidelity.

Penelope was the daughter of the Spartan prince Icarius and the nymph Periboea. Icarius's brother Tyndareos arranged Penelope's marriage to Odysseus in return for Odysseus's advice on the selection of a husband for his daughter Helen.

Following the wedding, Icarius pleaded with Penelope to stay. However, by drawing her veil over her face, Penelope signaled that her new life was with Odysseus. Icarius dedicated a statue to Modesty on the spot where she stood, and the newlyweds began their life together on the island of Ithaca.

Odysseus and Penelope had not been married long before the Trojan prince Paris's abduction of Helen incited the Greeks to go to war with Troy. The conflict lasted 10 years and only ended when the Greeks used trickery to breach the Trojans' walls. After their victory, the various Greek leaders sailed back to their respective cities. However, Odysseus's journey home was long and arduous—it was only after 10 more years and numerous adventures that he finally arrived back in Ithaca.

Penelope and the suitors

Penelope never gave up hope that her husband would return safely. However, most people assumed that he was dead and expected Penelope to remarry. In the months following the end of the Trojan War, more than 100 suitors from all over Greece traveled to Ithaca to seek Penelope's hand in marriage, setting up camp at Penelope's home. Try as she might, Penelope could not persuade them to leave. After six or seven years of being put off by Penelope, the suitors finally demanded that she select a husband. She announced that she must first complete a burial blanket for Odysseus's father. For three years Penelope wove her blanket during the day and secretly unwove her progress at night so that the work would never be completed. Finally, however, one of her handmaidens betrayed her to the suitors.

At this point Odysseus arrived back in Ithaca. When the goddess Athena warned him of the situation at his palace, Odysseus disguised himself as a beggar and visited Penelope, who did not recognize her husband. However, his assertion that he had met Odysseus on his travels filled her with new hope. Penelope told the beggar of her next diversionary tactic. She would announce that the suitor who could stretch Odysseus's bow and shoot an arrow through 12 ax handles set in a row would become her new husband. Penelope knew that no one but Odysseus himself could accomplish this feat.

All the suitors tried in vain. Odysseus, however, completed the task with ease. He then threw off his

Happy and Unhappy Endings

Our main source for the story of Odysseus and Penelope is the *Odyssey*, an epic poem written by Greek poet Homer. The work concludes with the joyous reunion of Penelope and Odysseus. However, other versions of Penelope's story end less happily. Apollodorus (fl. 140 BCE), a Greek prose writer, records several of these alternate endings. In one version of the story, Penelope was seduced by Antinous, the most unpleasant of the suitors, and returned by Odysseus to her father. In another version, Penelope surrendered to the sexual advances of Amphinomus, another suitor, and Odysseus killed her for being unfaithful. In other versions of the myth, the enchantress Circe, whom Odysseus met on his travels, bore him a son named Telegonus, who accidentally killed Odysseus in Ithaca. Penelope later married Telegonus, whereupon Circe granted the pair of them immortality. Some of these alternate endings paint Penelope in a morally questionable light. However, the most enduring image of Penelope is that of the steadfast wife and mother in Homer's *Odyssey*.

Above: This fresco by Italian artist Pinturicchio (1454–1531) depicts Penelope being harassed by suitors while weaving at her loom. In the background a ship returns Odysseus to his home island.

disguise and, with the help of his son Telemachus and some faithful servants, slaughtered all of the suitors. Odysseus then sent for Penelope. Still not believing that her husband had really returned, Penelope demanded that their bed be moved out of their bedroom. Odysseus protested that the bed, built with a living tree as one of the bedposts, could not be moved. Thus Odysseus passed Penelope's final test to prove his identity and the pair were happily reunited.

Penelope in art and literature

Penelope has been a popular subject in various artistic media. Vases and relief sculptures have borne her image since the fifth century BCE, and artists have painted scenes of her, Odysseus, and Telemachus since the 1500s. In the 20th century she appeared in the opera *Pénélope* by Gabriel Fauré (1845–1924) and the ballet *Odyssey* by George Couroupos (b. 1942).

The story of Penelope and Odysseus is told at greatest length by Greek poet Homer (c. ninth–eighth century BCE) in the *Odyssey*, an account of Odysseus's travels after the Trojan War. Historians are divided about the extent to which Homer's stories are based on real events and people. Pausanias, a Greek geographer living in the second century CE, claims to have visited the site of the statue to Modesty and the site of Penelope's tomb on his travels. It is more likely, however, that Penelope was created by Homer as the representation of a model Greek wife. No matter what the truth, Penelope's character is echoed throughout literature in portrayals of women whose faithfulness cannot be shaken.

DEBORAH THOMAS

Bibliography

Homer, and Robert Fagles, trans. *The Odyssey*. New York: Penguin USA, 1999.
Howatson, M. C., and Ian Chilvers. *Concise Oxford Companion to Classical Literature*. New York: Oxford University Press, 1993.

SEE ALSO: Athena; Circe; Helen; Odysseus.

PERSEPHONE

Persephone was the Greek goddess of agriculture and the underworld. She was daughter of Demeter, goddess of grain, and Zeus, king of the gods. Her name took many forms, including Proserpina in Latin and Proserpine in English.

Persephone was abducted by Hades, her uncle and god of the underworld, to be his wife. Angry and distraught at her daughter's disappearance, Demeter first made the earth barren, and then wandered weeping through the world until she discovered Persephone's location and demanded that the girl be returned to her. Zeus persuaded Hades to give up Persephone, but before Hades let her go, he forced her to eat six pomegranate seeds. The fruit was sacred to Hades, and for that reason Persephone was forever obliged to return to her husband for several months of every year, during fall and winter. While Persephone was below ground, nothing grew on earth, but fertility returned when she was reunited with her mother in spring.

Homeric Hymn

The earliest detailed account of the myth of Persephone is found in the Homeric Hymns (works in the style of Homer, but written long after his death). In the "Hymn to Demeter"

Right: This Greek statue of Persephone on her throne dates from the sixth century BCE.

(sixth century BCE), Hades swoops down on Persephone and carries her off to his realm below. Hearing her cries, Demeter searches everywhere before hearing of her daughter's fate from Helios, the sun god. On learning that Zeus was behind the abduction, Demeter withdraws from divine society. In her wanderings she arrives at Eleusis—a Greek city on the Saronic Gulf about 13 miles (21 km) northwest of Athens—disguised as an old woman. There the daughters of King Celeus take her home to care for their baby brother Demophon. At first the royal infant thrives, anointed with ambrosia by her divine nurse, but when his mother, Metaneira, sees Demeter holding the baby in a fire in an effort to make him immortal, she screams in fright. The offended goddess drops the baby and announces that now Demophon will be subject to death like all other mortals. Demeter then orders the people of Eleusis to build a temple in her honor, and she promises to teach them mystery rites.

Enraged by her double loss, Demeter withdraws to her temple, and for an entire year no crops grow on earth. Famine looms, and the gods, concerned that the annihilation of mortals will lead to the loss of sacrifices, intervene. Every deity comes in turn to Demeter, but she will not be swayed until Hermes brings Persephone back to her. Mother and daughter are reunited, but their joy is allayed to some extent when Persephone tells Demeter that she has eaten pomegranate seeds. As a result, the year is henceforth divided into a time of barrenness and a time of fertility, which the hymn explicitly connects with the coming of spring.

Right: In this 19th-century bookplate, Persephone is so hungry that she eats some pomegranate seeds, thus sealing her own fate.

Persephone and the Seasons

The period of Persephone's annual withdrawal to the underworld is usually correlated with winter, and the period of her return with spring. The Homeric Hymn makes this explicit. However, this does not exactly correspond with the climatic realities of Greece, where the heat of the summer makes it the barren time of the year. Nonetheless, it seems that the ancient Greeks interpreted the myth's seasonal chronology much as we do today. This has caused some scholars to suggest that the myth may have originated in a more northern climate and was adopted by the Greeks, although such speculations are difficult to prove.

In its simplest form, the myth of Persephone and Demeter symbolizes the origin of the seasons, but it has several other layers of meaning. In some versions of the legend, Demeter also bestows the secrets of agriculture on mortals as a token of her gratitude for their help in the search for Persephone. The hymn itself assumes that agriculture is already well known at the time of the myth, and that the goddess's grief and anger disrupt it. Because Demeter's contribution to human life is the technique of crop cultivation, scholars have assumed that earlier versions of the myth are the ones that explain the origins of agriculture. The hymn also explains the origins of the Eleusinian Mysteries and has often been used to try to interpret details of those rites.

In psychological readings, the myth represents the struggle of a mother and daughter to come to terms with the separation brought about by the latter's marriage. In some versions of the legend, the power of patriarchy is made explicit: Zeus wants to marry Persephone off to his brother and does not consult her mother before doing so. It is only after Demeter has been reassured that Hades will be a good husband and that her daughter will not lack for honor that she is reconciled to the union. Persephone's awakening

sexuality and the pull of divided loyalties are evident in the hymn's two different versions of the episode of the pomegranate seeds . The first contains nothing about coercion, but in the second Persephone tells her mother that Hades forced her to eat the seeds. Since Homeric style allows for the exact repetition of lengthy passages, this variation is significant. It may suggest the daughter's reluctance to admit to her mother that she is not an entirely unwilling bride. The pomegranate conventionally symbolizes death and eternal life, but here the eating of the seeds also suggests sex and procreation.

A timid young girl in the Homeric Hymn, Persephone is elsewhere a fearsome queen of the underworld. In the *Odyssey* by Homer (c. ninth–eighth century BCE), the hero Odysseus fears that if he lingers in the underworld Persephone will send a Gorgon against him. Persephone also becomes involved in a romantic triangle that is oddly reminiscent of her own situation. The goddess Aphrodite falls in love with the beautiful young Adonis. When he is killed by a boar, Persephone, who has also fallen in love with him, refuses to let him leave the underworld. Eventually a compromise is arranged: Adonis will spend half the year with her and half the year with his other divine lover.

Persephone in art

The myth of Persephone was often depicted in Greek and Roman art. The abduction was also the subject of *The Rape of Proserpina* by Roman poet Claudian (c. 370–c. 404 CE). Although extremely popular in Latin literature, the legend of Persephone did not become widespread in Western

Pomegranate Symbolism

In many cultures both the pomegranate itself and various objects that represent it symbolize abundance and fertility. The red precious gemstone garnet is an aluminum silicate that derives its name from its resemblance to the seed of the pomegranate. When worn as jewelry, garnet symbolizes fecundity, and it is one of the traditional gifts from a husband to his wife on the occasion of their second wedding anniversary. In the Christian church, the fruit itself and references to it are often used to stand for the Resurrection, immortality, royalty, and fertility.

In ancient Anatolia (a region of modern Turkey), the pomegranate was a sacred fruit of paradise. There it was believed that scattering pomegranate fruit inside the house of a newlywed bride would make her marriage long-lasting and productive, as well as making the family rich, with many children who will have long life.

In Rome, the goddess Juno was often shown holding a pomegranate as a symbol of marriage. In heraldry, the pomegranate was the badge of Catherine of Aragon, first wife of English king Henry VIII.

Above: In this painting of hell by the French artist François de Nome (1593–1634), Persephone sits on her underworld throne next to her husband, Hades.

literature and art until the 17th century. Flemish painter Peter Paul Rubens (1577–1640) and Italian sculptor Gian Lorenzo Bernini (1598–1680) both created representations of her in the early 1620s. In the 19th century poets such as A. C. Swinburne (1837–1909) and painters such as Dante Gabriel Rossetti (1828–1882) and Frederick Leighton (1830–1896) drew on her myth in numerous works. In the 20th century the myth was attractive to a wide range of women writers, including American H. D. (Hilda Doolittle) (1886–1961) and Canadian Margaret Atwood (born 1939).

DEBORAH LYONS

Bibliography
Bulfinch, Thomas. *Bulfinch's Mythology.* New York: Modern Library, 1998.
Howatson, M. C., and Ian Chilvers. *Concise Oxford Companion to Classical Literature.* New York: Oxford University Press, 1993.

SEE ALSO: Demeter; Earth Mother; Fertility; Greece; Hades; Mystery Cults; Zeus.

PERSEUS

In Greek mythology, Perseus was famous above all for two great feats: slaying the Gorgon Medusa and rescuing the African princess Andromeda from a sea monster.

The story of Perseus is one of the most popular Greek legends. It has been retold many times, notably by Greek poets Homer (c. ninth–eighth century BCE) and Hesiod (fl. 800 BCE), and by Roman poet Ovid (43 BCE–17 CE). Because there are so many literary sources, there are numerous different versions, some of which are mutually contradictory. In outline, however, the story is as follows. Perseus was the son of Zeus and Danae, daughter of King Acrisius of Argos, a city of the Peloponnese peninsula in southern Greece. The Delphic oracle warned the king that he would be slain by his own grandson. At the time of the prophecy, Danae was not even pregnant. In an effort to prevent the inevitable, Acrisius locked up his daughter in an underground chamber made of brass or stone with only a single, tiny aperture for light and air. Her sole companion was a nurse. In later accounts, Danae's prison became a bronze tower. The earliest work in which this version appears is the *Odes* of Roman poet Horace (65–8 BCE).

Divine intervention

What the oracle had not mentioned, however, was that the father of Acrisius's grandchild would be Zeus, the most powerful of all Greek deities, against whom resistance was useless. When the time was ripe, the chief god came through the roof of Danae's cell in a shower of gold. The fruit of their union was Perseus. When Acrisius discovered the child, he tried to save himself by locking Danae and Perseus inside a chest, which he cast into the sea. Zeus, however, would not let his offspring drown. He watched over the chest until it drifted close to the shore of Seriphos, an island in the Aegean Sea. There it was noticed by a fisherman, Dictes. He caught the chest in his net,

released its occupants, and took them to his brother, Polydectes, king of the island. The monarch received the woman and her baby son hospitably and let them live in peace on his island.

Before long Polydectes fell in love with Danae, but his desire for her was inhibited by the fact that she already had a child. As Perseus grew up, there was increasing tension between him and his mother's suitor. In an effort to rid himself of Perseus, Polydectes hatched a complicated plot. He announced his marriage to Danae and demanded a wedding gift from all the warriors of the kingdom. He anticipated, correctly, that Perseus, who by this time had grown into a man, would want to bring the most lavish present of all to his mother's wedding. So when Perseus asked Polydectes if he had anything in mind as a gift, the king suggested the head of the Gorgon Medusa, a fearsome monster who could turn men to stone with a single look. Naturally Polydectes thought that such a task was impossible—the monster would kill Perseus, and he and Danae would be left alone together.

Polydectes, however, underestimated the determination and resourcefulness of his bride-to-be's son. Perseus went about his task with a will, first visiting the Graeae, sisters and guardians of the Gorgon. These three witches, who were the daughters of Phorcys and Ceto, were gray-haired from birth and shared only one eye and one tooth among them. Their names were Deino ("dread"), Enyo ("horror"), and Pemphredo ("alarm"). Perseus elicited from them the secret whereabouts of the Gorgon—thought by some writers to have been a cave in a remote part of northern Africa, in a land that is now part of Libya—by stealing their one eye, which he used as a bargaining tool. As he left the Graeae he also stole some magical aids that would prove vital to his quest—a helmet of darkness that rendered the wearer invisible, a pair of winged sandals, and a reflecting shield. (In other versions of the story, Perseus was given the helmet by Hades, the sandals by Hermes, and the shield by Athena). Thus armed, Perseus tracked down the Gorgon and slew her while she slept. He took care not to look at Medusa directly—which would have been his death—but

Right: This ancient Roman fresco depicts Perseus freeing Andromeda from her chains in time to save her from Poseidon's sea monster.

approached her by walking backward and looking only at her image reflected in his highly polished bronze shield. He cut off her hideous, snake-covered head with a sickle and took it with him as a trophy.

African excursion

With Medusa's head in his possession, Perseus now had the power to turn anything to stone, and on his way home he used it to transform the giant Atlas into a mountain. (However, this contradicts another story in which Heracles—a descendant of Perseus—encounters the giant on his return from the garden of the Hesperides.) Continuing his journey flying over Ethiopia with his winged sandals, or, according to some accounts, on the winged horse Pegasus, Perseus noticed a maiden tied to a rock in the sea, naked except for her jewelry, while two anguished people watched her from the shore. Perseus landed beside the couple, Cepheus and Cassiopeia, who told him that they were sacrificing their daughter, Andromeda, to atone for Cassiopeia's sin of boasting that their only child was more beautiful

Pegasus

According to some versions of the legend, when Perseus cut off Medusa's head, the beautiful winged horse Pegasus sprang from the Gorgon's neck. In other accounts, the stallion was created by Poseidon from drops of Medusa's blood that had fallen into the realm of the sea god.

By all accounts, as soon as he was born, Pegasus flew across the Mediterranean Sea from northern Africa to Mount Helicon in Corinth on mainland Greece. There he struck the earth with his hoof and caused the Hippocrene fountain to flow. The waters of this spring came to be regarded as a source of artistic inspiration and were sacred to the Muses. As a result, Pegasus, too, was strongly linked with literary creativity. In other myths, the horse served Zeus faithfully as the carrier of his thunder and lightning; he also became the favorite mount of Apollo and the Muses.

Pegasus was eventually tamed by the hero Bellerophon, who broke the horse using a golden bridle given to him by Athena. When Bellerophon was sent to destroy the fire-breathing dragon Chimaera, which had been ravaging the Lycian countryside, he rode Pegasus above the dragon's reach and was able to kill her.

Early Corinthians inscribed some of their coins with the figure of Pegasus. To Romans, Pegasus was a symbol of immortality.

Left: This painting by British artist Frederick Leighton (1830–1896) shows Perseus riding Pegasus to the rescue of Andromeda.

than the Nereids, sea nymphs and daughters of Poseidon. Poseidon, angered by this affront, had sent first a flood to ravage the kingdom, and then a sea monster that fed on human flesh. Desperate, Cepheus and Cassiopeia consulted an oracle, who told them that the only way to appease the sea god was to sacrifice their daughter to his monster. They promised Perseus that he could marry the girl if he could only save her. No sooner had they finished speaking than the monster broke the surface of the waves and bore down on Andromeda. Perseus flew over to the rock and decapitated the monster with a single blow of his sickle. In some versions of the legend, Poseidon later turned the body of the monster into the sea's first coral.

Andromeda fell in love with her rescuer and wanted to marry him. However, she was already betrothed to another, Agenor. On the day of the wedding between Perseus and Andromeda, Agenor and his henchmen turned up uninvited, disrupting the ceremony and demanding that Andromeda be released from the bargain. Reneging on their earlier promise, Cepheus and Cassiopeia sided with Agenor because he was the son of a powerful neighboring king. When Perseus insisted that the wedding go ahead, Agenor tried to abduct Andromeda, while his friends attacked Perseus. Perseus took out Medusa's head from the bag in which he kept it and turned Agenor and his gang to stone. He also transformed Cepheus and Cassiopeia, so that Cassiopeia was punished for her sin of pride. Perseus flew off with Andromeda in his arms.

Unfinished business

When Perseus reached Seriphos, he discovered that, in his absence, Polydectes had mistreated his mother. The hostility between the couple seems to have arisen from Danae's desire to delay the wedding until her son's return; the king wanted to go ahead with the wedding because he knew—or thought he knew—that they would wait forever. Perseus confronted the king, and as they argued it dawned on the young man that the purpose of the Gorgon mission had been to kill him. Incensed, he held up the Gorgon's head: as soon as Polydectes set eyes on her face, he turned to stone. Perseus was reunited with Danae, and they decided to return to Argos. Before they left, Perseus gave Medusa's head to the goddess Athena, who placed it on her shield or breastplate.

Below: This ancient Roman statue of Perseus depicts the hero holding the head of the Gorgon Medusa.

Perseus in Art

The exploits of Perseus have been a popular theme for artists throughout the Common Era. Two of the most distinguished works on the subject are *Perseus Releases Andromeda* by Flemish master Peter Paul Rubens (1577–1640) and *The Arming of Perseus* by British painter Edward Burne-Jones (1833–1898). Both paintings adapt the Perseus legend to the artist's own purposes. Rubens depicts Perseus mounted on the winged horse Pegasus, even though most literary versions of the tale suggest that the hero flew with the aid of winged sandals. Burne-Jones, on the other hand, ignores the tradition that the Graeae were old and ugly. Instead, he portrays the three sisters as classic Pre-Raphaelite beauties.

Below: In Edward Burne-Jones's painting, Perseus does not steal the winged sandals but is given them by the Graeae, who are neither old nor ugly but young and beautiful.

Acrisius meets his fate

On their return to Argos, Perseus, Danae, and Andromeda were welcomed home by King Acrisius. The king had not forgotten about the oracle, but he was glad finally to have a male heir. He saw that Perseus was a fine young man and found it impossible to imagine him committing murder. Some time later, however, Perseus went to Larissa, a city in Thessaly in east-central Greece, to participate in a discus contest at some funeral games. One of his throws accidentally struck the head of a spectator and killed him—when Perseus went to try to help his victim, he discovered that it was Acrisius. The Delphic oracle's prophecy had been fulfilled. In other versions of the legend, on hearing of Perseus's imminent return, Acrisius fled to Thessaly to escape the fate prophesied by the oracle. Perseus followed him there, but had no hostility toward his grandfather: his death was still an accident. Given the manner of Acrisius's death, Perseus was uneasy about succeeding his grandfather, so he exchanged thrones with the king of Tiryns and Mycenae, two great Bronze Age cities of the Peloponnese. In later life, Perseus and Andromeda had seven children—six sons and a daughter, Gorgophone, who became infamous for refusing to follow the Greek custom of committing suicide after the death of her first husband. When Perseus died, he was placed by his grieving father Zeus in the night sky, where he became a constellation visible in winter to observers in the northern hemisphere. In it he appears with sword upraised and the head of the slain Gorgon Medusa on his outstretched hand.

KATHLEEN JENKS

Bibliography

Hesiod, and M. L. West, trans. *Theogony; and Works and Days*. New York: Oxford University Press, 1999.

Howatson, M. C., and Ian Chilvers. *Concise Oxford Companion to Classical Literature*. New York: Oxford University Press, 1993.

SEE ALSO: Andromeda; Bellerophon; Danae; Gorgons; Hades; Heracles; Hermes; Poseidon; Zeus.

PHAETHON

In Greek mythology, Phaethon—whose name means "shining" or "radiant one"—was the son of the nymph Clymene. He did not know who his father was, and when he asked his mother, she told him that he was the child of Helios, the sun god.

Phaethon assumed that Clymene had told him the truth about his father's identity, but when his schoolfriend Epaphus mockingly doubted his paternity, he went back to his mother and demanded proof. She told him to go and ask Helios himself; she directed him to seek out his father in India, the land where the sun rises.

The answer and the promise

When Phaethon arrived at the sun god's palace, he stood amazed. Everything from the columns to the doors, which were engraved by Vulcan himself, was fashioned in gold, silver, bronze, and ivory. Helios was reclining on a throne of emeralds and surrounded by gods and goddesses who represented the passage of time. When Phaethon asked Helios whether he was his father, the sun god replied that not only was he the boy's father, but that he would also grant Phaethon whatever his heart desired. Phaethon thought for a moment before asking to drive his father's chariot, the vehicle that brought the sun to the world every morning at dawn. Helios saw the danger and pleaded with Phaethon to change his mind. "Look at the worry in my face," he pleaded. "Hear the concern in my voice: they should be proof enough of my love for you." He went on to say that the horses were too difficult even for Zeus to control, and that the path through the sky was dangerous and filled with monsters such as the Scorpion, the Lion, the Bull, and the Crab. Helios begged Phaethon to ask for anything else, but Phaethon was determined to attempt the impossible. Helios realized that he must comply with his request because he had sworn by the Styx River to grant Phaethon's wish, and not even a god could break such a solemn promise.

Distraught, Helios gave Phaethon all the advice he could, then rubbed a magic ointment on his face to protect

Above: This 17th-century Italian oil painting depicts the fateful meeting between Phaethon and his long-lost father, Helios.

Celestial Science

Despite the moral lessons to be learned from Phaethon's tragedy, his story may have a deeper scientific significance. For example, scholars such as Diodorus Siculus (90–21 BCE) of Rome connected Phaethon's story with the creation of the Milky Way. The streak of stars was clearly visible in the dark skies of the ancient world, and the story helped to explain it.

Some scientists have also questioned whether the legend arose because of Earth's contact with a comet or meteor. Others have suggested that the myth might have resulted from a particularly dry period. Ancient people could have interpreted either phenomena as the consequence of the chariot of the sun coming too close to Earth. Stories from ancient Mesoamerica and China both suggest a dry period between 1200 and 1000 BCE. Whether a natural phenomenon lies at the root of this myth or not, one thing is certain: the effects of such an event were extremely troubling, especially in a world with limited understanding of meteorology.

him from the intensity of the sunlight. No sooner had Phaethon set off than the horses realized that their usual driver was not at the reins. When Phaethon passed the Scorpion in the sky, he was frightened and dropped the reins. The horses ran out of control, wildly galloping first high, then low, dragging the sun across mountaintops and valleys, setting fire to everything in their path. Not only did mountains and cities catch fire, but also rivers, springs, and fields of crops. According to Ovid (43 BCE–17 CE), the Latin poet who tells this story in its entirety in the *Metamorphoses*, Phaethon's chariot ride blackened the skin of Ethiopians, created the Libyan Desert, and caused the Nile River to hide its head in the sand.

When earth goddess Gaia could take no more of this destruction, she cried out to Zeus to intervene. The chief god struck the chariot with a bolt of lightning, and Phaethon plummeted to his death into a river, later said to

Below: The Fall of Phaethon *by Luca Giordano (1632-1705).*

Right: This 16th-century Italian painting depicts the moment when the Heliades, Phaethon's sisters, mourning his death, begin to turn into trees.

have been the Eridanus (the modern Po in northern Italy). Helios himself mourned for a day, during which the sun was not seen in the sky. According to Ovid, Helios shirked his light-bringing responsibility out of anger at Zeus, who, he asserted, could not have handled the chariot any better than Phaethon. It was only after other gods and goddesses interceded that Helios resumed his duties, but not before savagely beating his horses for their part in his son's death.

Meanwhile, nymphs in the service of Hesperus (the Evening Star) found and buried Phaethon's body. When they did so, two miraculous transformations took place. First, Cycnus was so distraught by the death of his friend Phaethon that the gods took pity on him and placed him in the stars as a swan (the constellation Cygnus). The second transformation was that of Phaethon's sisters, the Heliades. Having mourned their brother at his tomb on the banks of the river, the Heliades attempted to rise, but their bodies were no longer human. Where there had formerly been skin, bark grew. Their legs became rooted to the ground, their arms turned into boughs, and leaves sprouted from the tops of their heads. Clymene, their mother, attempted to tear the bark away, but the girls cried out in agony. As their bodies were changed into poplar trees, their tears turned to amber, a precious gemstone that was worn by Roman brides. In Ovid's account, the tomb of Phaethon was forever shaded by poplar trees:

"Here Phaethon lies, his father's charioteer—
Great was his fall, yet did he greatly dare."

Explanatory theories

Phaethon's story may have its origins in explanations of climatic or astronomical phenomena, such as those that are thought to occur when Earth passes through the tail of a comet. However, it can also be interpreted as a warning against the impulsiveness of youth. If it had not been for his stubbornness, insatiable curiosity, and refusal to heed his father's warnings, Phaethon might not have died in such violent and tragic circumstances. His relentless ambition served as a reminder of the need for humility, and of the fact that humans were subservient and inferior to the gods. This story, like that of Daedalus and Icarus, was used to illustrate what can happen to children who disobey their parents' wishes.

Later, scholars during the Renaissance also interpreted this story as a warning, but this time in a Christian context: the moral was that humans should not strive to be too close to God, which was, after all, Lucifer's mistake. It was also during this period in Europe that Phaethon became an inspiration for artists, most notably in a work by Peter Paul Rubens (1577–1640). Phaethon's name has survived in modern English usage, where a phaeton is a four-wheeled, horse-drawn vehicle and, more recently, a model of Volkswagen automobile.

ANTHONY BULLOCH

Bibliography

Howatson, M. C., and Ian Chilvers. *Concise Oxford Companion to Classical Literature.* New York: Oxford University Press, 1993.
Ovid, and A. D. Melville, trans. *Metamorphoses.* New York: Oxford University Press, 1998.

SEE ALSO: Daedalus; Helios; Icarus; Zeus.

PHILOCTETES

In Greek mythology, Philoctetes was the hero to whom Heracles entrusted his famous bow and poisoned arrows. He used these weapons to shoot Paris, whose death played a major part in the Greeks' final victory in the Trojan War.

Philoctetes was the son of Demonassa and Poeas, king of the Malians, a people who inhabited part of southern Thessaly, a region of mainland Greece near Mount Oeta, to the northwest of Athens between Epirus and the Aegean Sea. Etymologically, the name Philoctetes means "one who likes to acquire things," and as a young man he received one of the most famous gifts in Greek legend: the bow and arrows that had formerly belonged to Heracles, which in most versions the hero gave Philoctetes as a reward for lighting his funeral pyre.

When the Greeks under Agamemnon set sail from the mainland port of Aulis at the start of the Trojan War, they were warned by an oracle that, on their way across the Aegean Sea, they must stop on an island and sacrifice at the altar of a deity named Chryse. Only one of the sailors on board the flotilla knew where to find this shrine— Philoctetes, who in his youth had been present at a sacrifice offered there by Heracles.

The Greeks eventually landed on the island. As they approached the open-air altar, Philoctetes was bitten on the foot by a serpent. The wound would not heal, and Philoctetes' cries of pain made it impossible for the Greeks to perform the sacrifice, which needed to be carried out in silence. The odor of his wound was also offensive, so they took him to the neighboring island of Lemnos, put him ashore, and sailed for Troy.

Crucial comeback

In the ninth year of the Trojan War, the Trojans had the upper hand. Either Helenus or Calchas prophesied to the Greeks that Troy could be taken only if four conditions

---

The Death of Heracles

Heracles won Iole, daughter of King Eurytus of Oechalia by beating the king in an archery contest, but was not awarded his prize. He later avenged this injustice by killing the king and taking Iole as his concubine, although by then he was married to Deianeira. When he returned from Oechalia his jealous wife decided to try to win her husband back by using a love charm. What she thought was a love charm, however, was actually a deadly poison. Years before, the centaur Nessus had tried to rape her and was killed by one of Heracles' arrows. As he died, he gave Deianeira his bloodstained robe, telling her that it was an aphrodisiac. The blood on the robe had been poisoned by the venom from the Lernean Hydra, into which Heracles had dipped his arrows. Deianeira innocently gave Heracles the fatal garment. After putting it on, Heracles felt a searing pain. He tore the robe off, and his flesh came off with it. Thus trapped painfully between life and death, Heracles bravely opted for the latter. With his son Hyllus, Heracles built

a funeral pyre on top of Mount Oeta and clambered to the top of it. None of his friends and family, however, could bear to light the pyre. Philoctetes chanced upon this gathering and was persuaded by Heracles to light the pyre in exchange for his bow and arrows. The mortal part of Heracles burned away, and Philoctetes took possession of the magical weapons.

Like most Greek kings of the generation that lived through the Trojan War, Philoctetes is said in some versions to have vied for Helen's hand and swore to her father, Tyndareos, that he would support Helen's husband, whoever he was, in the event of any calamity involving her. After Helen was seized by Paris and taken to Troy, Tyndareos called in the oaths. Each of the former suitors arrived with reinforcements to help Helen's husband, Menelaus, recapture her. According to Homer, Philoctetes led seven ships from the Malians and Olizonians, although during the war he was afflicted with a terrible wound that necessitated his absence from battle.

were met: first, that Achilles' son Neoptolemus fight for the Greeks; second, that Pelops's bones be brought to Troy; third, that the Palladium (a small wooden statue of Pallas Athena that was supposed to safeguard Troy) be stolen from the city; and finally that Heracles's bow and arrows be used against Troy.

In order to satisfy the fourth requirement, Odysseus returned to Lemnos, where he found Philoctetes living in squalor and using the bow and arrow to hunt birds for food. Philoctetes had no desire to help the Greeks—after all, it was they who had marooned him there in the first place. So Odysseus persuaded his companion, Neoptolemus, whom Philoctetes had never met, to trick the castaway into giving up his weapons. The plan worked, but Neoptolemus then had a change of heart and insisted that they rescue Philoctetes. Odysseus was undecided, but Heracles, now a god, appeared and directed the outcome. Philoctetes accompanied the Greeks back to Troy, where he killed Paris.

Different sources give varying accounts of Philoctetes' fate after the Trojan War. According to Greek poet Homer (c. ninth–eighth century BCE), he returned to Thessaly; but according to Greek playwright Apollodorus (third century BCE) and Roman poet Virgil (70–19 BCE), he journeyed to southern Italy, where he founded the city of Petelia in Lucania. He is also said to have built a temple to Apollo the Wanderer, where he dedicated his magical bow and arrows. Most accounts agree, however, that Philoctetes was killed in battle.

Variant accounts

That is the bare outline of the story of Philoctetes. The details have been fleshed out by numerous writers since antiquity, thus giving rise to many variant versions. For example, according to some authors, it was not Philoctetes himself who lit Heracles' funeral pyre but his father, Poeas, who later bequeathed the bow and arrows to his son. Several writers—notably Roman epic poet Valerius Flaccus (first century CE)—state that Philoctetes was one of the sailors who accompanied Jason on his quest for the Golden Fleece. However, Apollonius of Rhodes (third century BCE), the traditional source of the story of the Argonauts, does not mention him aboard the *Argo*.

The Trojan War occurred a generation after Jason's voyage, and it was mainly the sons of the Argonauts who led the Greek forces to Troy. Philoctetes

Left: This statue by French sculptor Jean-Baptiste Carpeaux (1827–1875) shows Philoctetes as he is bitten by the serpent.

Philoctetes' Wound

There are several different accounts of the way in which Philoctetes acquired his festering wound. According to Proclus (c. 410–485 CE), Greek philosopher and author of a summary of the Trojan War, Philoctetes was bitten by a snake on the island of Tenedos while the Greeks were feasting there. Apollodorus (third century BCE) had previously stated that this happened during a sacrifice to Athena or Apollo. Sophocles instead locates this event at the temple of the nymph Chryse on an island of the same name that was said to have subsequently been submerged beneath the sea. Neither Sophocles nor any other writer gave a precise location for the island, but it was generally assumed to have been near Lemnos. The wound never healed, causing Philoctetes immense pain and altering his whole life. Henceforth he was driven psychologically into a middle ground between life and death—his fate is thus similar to that of Heracles after he had come into contact with the Hydra's venom.

In the account of the life of Philoctetes given by Servius Tullius (578–534 BCE), Philoctetes had promised Heracles that he would never tell anyone where to find his grave. When pressed for the information, however, Philoctetes marked the place by stamping his foot. While he was doing this one of the deadly arrows fell loose of the quiver, pricking his foot. The wound putrefied, and eventually Philoctetes' comrades could no longer bear to hear his continual moaning. They marooned him on nearby Lemnos, a place also associated with other smelly things in mythology—the divine blacksmith Hephaestus and the Lemnian women, who were cursed with a strange body odor.

Below: The adder or viper is thought to have been the poisonous serpent that bit Philoctetes on the foot.

was the only hero who is said to have taken part in both expeditions. In some versions of the legend, he is even said to have been one of the early suitors of Helen of Troy.

Many of the great ancient Greek dramatists are known to have written about the story of Philoctetes, but the only one of their works that survives is *Philoctetes* by Sophocles (c. 496–406 BCE). The speech in which the hero expresses his anguish at having been betrayed by those he regarded as his friends, and the scene in which he has contact with humans for the first time in almost a decade, make this play one of the most powerful in Western literature.

Although the story of Philoctetes is heroic and full of great achievements, the legendary figure became most famous for his suffering. This illustrates a common tendency in Greek mythology to balance great glory with great suffering in the lives of its heroes. The character of Philoctetes has become an archetype of the misunderstood and abused genius whose assistance becomes essential to the survival of his people in times of adversity.

KATHRYN CHEW

Bibliography

Bulfinch, Thomas. *Bulfinch's Mythology.* New York: Modern Library, 1998.

Graves, Robert. *The Greek Myths.* New York: Penguin USA, 1993.

Homer, and Robert Fagles, trans. *The Iliad.* New York: Penguin USA, 2003.

Sophocles, and Christopher Parry, ed. *Philoctetes.* London: Cambridge University Press, 1969.

SEE ALSO: Achilles; Apollo; Helen; Hephaestus; Heracles; Jason; Odysseus; Paris.

PHOBOS

Phobos, Greek god of fear, was the son of Aphrodite, the goddess of sensual love and beauty, and her lover Ares, the self-centered, drunken, and dim-witted god of war. Phobos's twin brother was Deimos, or dread. Phobos's name is the root of the modern word *phobia*.

Above: A fresco from the House of Saints and Martyrs in the Roman city of Pompeii depicts Aphrodite with her lover Ares. Their twins, Phobos and Deimos, inherited their father's warlike nature.

Phobos shared with most of Ares' other children a terrible reputation that always preceded him. There are few occasions when Phobos plays a major role in mythology, but there are numerous references to his presence in ancient Greek literature, such as in Hesiod's (fl. 800 BCE) epics *Theogony* and *Shield of Heracles,* and also in Homer's (c. ninth–eighth century BCE) epic the *Iliad.*

Some mythographers suggest that Ares was originally a death god before he became the god of war. He underwent this transition because ancient Greeks were empire builders, constantly battling to extend their territory, and contemporary Greek culture associated death with war. The role of a death god differed little from a war god. However, the underworld, where the dead reside, became such a vast and overcrowded place after so many wars and deaths that governing the dead souls came to require a dedicated god. Later, after further differentiation, Hades became ruler of the underworld and Ares became associated exclusively with war. A further tie between Ares and death lies in the fact that Phobos and Deimos (Fear and Terror) and Ares' sister, Eris (Strife), appear in Greek mythology as death demons as well as war demons. In one myth, soul-eating underworld spirits known as the Keres make their first appearance in Greek mythology on the battlefield in the company of Phobos, Eris, and other war demons allied with Ares. Mythographers also argue that ancient Greeks followed the Babylonian custom of giving gods' names to planets. They passed the red planet belonging to the Babylonian death god Nergal to Ares, god of war, thus forging a relationship between death and war in Ares' character. The red planet is now known as Mars, for the Roman god of war.

Other children of Ares

Most of Ares' children were terrible in some way: they were often dangerous, belligerent, and unruly. Cycnus, for example, beheaded passing strangers and stacked the heads to make a temple that he dedicated to his father. Another son of Ares was Diomedes, who met with a gruesome death. He was king of the Bistones, a warlike tribe that lived in the ancient Greek region of Thrace. He kept four horses that he chained up and fed with human flesh.

Sacrifices to Phobos

In several Greek myths heroes and heroines sacrifice to Ares and his children, including Phobos, to improve their chances of victory in battle. Appeasing Phobos was seen to be a way of winning his favor so that opponents might suffer from the fear and panic that he could inflict upon them. In one myth the Amazon warrior Oreithyia sacrificed to Ares before she led an attack on Attica, where Theseus held captive her sister Antiope. To improve his chances in battle, Theseus was advised by an oracle to sacrifice to Phobos. After a four-month battle during which Antiope was slain, Theseus finally defeated the Amazons and Oreithyia retreated, to die of grief at her sister's death.

The Macedonian king and general Alexander the Great (356–323 BCE) also sacrificed to Phobos. Greek biographer Plutarch (c. 46–120 CE) reports that the sacrifice took place in the presence of a seer during a secret ritual the night before the battle of Arbela (331 BCE). Plutarch also mentions a sanctuary of Phobos in Sparta, which was closed during rare times of peace.

Left: The remains of a stone relief dating to the fifth century BCE depicting Queen Antiope of the Amazons and her abductor the Greek hero Theseus. He sacrificed to Phobos before defending Attica from Antiope's furious sister Oreithyia.

Diomedes died at the hands of Heracles, who had to tame the horses for his eighth labor. To calm and control the animals, Heracles fed Diomedes to them. The Amazon queen Penthesileia was a powerful and merciless daughter of Ares who led an army to defend Troy during the Trojan War. In some Greek myths Meleager is another of Ares' sons. He was the hero who killed a ravenous boar sent by the goddess of hunting, Artemis, who was angry that Oeneus, king of the Aetolians (who is sometimes credited as Meleager's father), had not sacrificed to her. During the Calydonian boar hunt, Meleager marshaled a band of men to hunt the beast and finally killed it himself. Harmonia was exceptional among Ares and Aphrodite's children. She was beautiful and virtuous and married Greek hero Cadmus; together they established the city of Thebes. Their wedding was so important that the gods attended and brought them gifts. In another version of the myth

Harmonia is a Naiad (water nymph) who is Ares' lover. The product of their union is the Amazons, a race of warrior women who live apart from men and fearlessly defend their way of life.

Phobos in mythology

In one myth Phobos features with another of Ares' sons, Kyknos, a renowned thief and highway bandit. The pair lay in wait for pilgrims traveling to Apollo's shrine at Pytho, beheaded them, and then stole the sacrificial oxen that the pilgrims were bringing to Apollo. One day, when the Greek hero Heracles approached the region in a chariot driven by his nephew Iolaus, they came upon another chariot in which Kyknos and his father Ares were riding with the twins Phobos and Deimos as their charioteers. (In some versions of the myth Phobos and Deimos are not charioteers for their father Ares, but are his horses, Fear and Terror). Kyknos took an instant dislike to Heracles and saw an opportunity to rid the world of the hero.

Heracles and Kyknos leaped from their chariots and began fighting. During the duel Heracles managed to sever two of Kyknos's neck tendons with his spear. As Kyknos fell mortally wounded, his enraged father jumped from

Phobos in the Stars

Ancient Greeks and later the Romans adopted astrology as a system to predict the future. The study of the position and movement of the planets was taken so seriously that astrologers often held important offices in the government, influencing politics with their advice. Astrology replaced more basic predictive systems such as reading the entrails of animals. It closely reflected contemporary pantheons so that Mars, the Roman counterpart of Ares, was associated with the red planet of the same name. Astronomy, the scientific study of the stars, adopted these Roman names and uses others from classical mythology to label new stars that are discovered.

In mid-August 1877 astronomers discovered two moons orbiting Mars. They were named Phobos and Deimos, the gods Fear and Dread, who were the sons of Mars, or Ares in Greek mythology. These names have proved ominous. The larger moon, Phobos, is so close to Mars that the planet's gravitational field is slowly claiming it. Scientists predict that, in 50 million years or so, Phobos will either crash to Mars' surface or shatter into a ring of debris circling the planet.

Above: An image of Phobos, one of the moons of the planet Mars, taken by a probe in 1978. The moon was named for the Greek god of fear, and son of Ares.

the chariot and continued the fight. The war god's spear struck hard against the shield of his opponent, knocking Heracles off balance. Tasting victory, Ares drew his sword and rushed to the kill. Heracles, however, managed to thrust his own spear deep into Ares' thigh and threw him to the ground. Phobos and Deimos leaped forward to snatch their injured father away and then fled to Olympus. Local Pythians eventually buried the body of Kyknos, but Apollo ordered the Anaurus River to wash away his grave, since he had attacked so many of his devotees and stolen their offerings.

Elsewhere in Greek mythology Phobos is represented metaphorically: he is not a personification of fear but fear itself. He is often referred to as an incapacitating fear that is free-floating, ungrounded, arising out of nowhere, illogical, and irrational. Ancient Greeks, especially soldiers during a battle, might feel the presence of Phobos and invoke his name to describe a fear that caused a rout or a terrified withdrawal. The feeling of fear associated with Phobos became a term described by his name, *phobos*. It has much in common with panic, which ancient Greeks called a *phobos panikos*, a *phobos* inflicted by the god of shepherds, Pan. Ancient Greeks sometimes viewed *phobos* as the result of the *mastix*, a whip or a metaphorical scourge that imposed mastery over animals but could also madden and disorder humans.

Modern phobias

All known phobias have their root in *phobos*. Some examples are phobophobia, fear of fear; claustrophobia, fear of enclosed spaces; agoraphobia, fear of open spaces; xenophobia, fear of strangers; aichomophobia, fear of being touched by a pointed object, whether a spear or an index finger; hagiophobia, fear of being around holy persons or objects; and cremnophobia, fear of falling off a cliff. Modern medical dictionaries list more than two hundred types of phobias.

Although Phobos was not a great deity in Greek mythology, the negative connotations of his name, many of which still exist today, ensure that he is one of the most enduring gods in the Greek pantheon.

KATHLEEN JENKS

Bibliography
Bulfinch, Thomas. *Bulfinch's Mythology.* New York: Modern Library, 1998.
Gardner, Jane F. *Roman Myths.* Austin, TX: University of Texas Press, 1994.
Homer, and Robert Fagles, trans. *The Iliad.* New York: Penguin USA, 2003.
Howatson, M. C., and Ian Chilvers. *Concise Oxford Companion to Classical Literature.* New York: Oxford University Press, 1993.

SEE ALSO: Apollo; Ares; Artemis; Diomedes; Heracles; Mars; Pan; Theseus.

PLANTS

Plants played a major role in the mythology and religious beliefs of many ancient cultures. Often certain plants were associated with particular gods and goddesses and were used in the rituals in which these deities were worshiped. Other plants were thought to have magical properties such as the ability to ward off evil—these beliefs often derived from a plant's unusual physical appearance or smell.

One of the most important ways in which plants played a part in the religious beliefs of ancient cultures was as symbols and manifestations of gods and goddesses. In Greek mythology, for example, Dionysus, god of wine and ecstasy, was associated with both grapes and ivy, while Demeter, the fertility goddess, was linked to corn. The Egyptian god Osiris, another fertility deity who in later times was worshiped as lord of the underworld, was also associated with corn. For both the ancient Greeks and Egyptians, corn symbolized death and rebirth, since it grew in summer and was harvested and planted again in winter. The story of Demeter's daughter, Persephone, parallels the agricultural cycle. She was kidnapped by Hades, the Greek ruler of the underworld, and thereafter spent much of the year below the earth as his queen. However, she came back to the earth for several months of the year, bringing fertility and growth to the world in spring and summer.

Another Greek deity who was heavily associated with a particular plant was Apollo, the Greek god of light. He was associated with the laurel tree, a connection that was explained by the story of his unrequited love for the nymph Daphne. Apollo chased Daphne, who prayed to her father, the river god Peneius, to rescue her. Peneius transformed his daughter into a laurel tree, which subsequently became sacred to Apollo.

Some scholars have suggested that priests at the oracle of Delphi might have interpreted the rustlings of a laurel tree as the voice of Apollo. This claim has been disputed. However, what is certain is that the laurel played a major part in the rituals performed at Delphi. Apollo's prophetess at

Left: The goddess Demeter, pictured here in a Roman mosaic, was strongly associated with corn. Corn was a symbol of fertility in many ancient cultures.

Delphi either chewed or burned laurel leaves in order to summon the god. The priestess then entered a trancelike state, in which she would contact Apollo.

Greek mythology is littered with many similar examples of people being transformed into either plants or trees. Roman poet Ovid (43 BCE–17 CE) wrote about many such transformations in his *Metamorphoses*. As well as the story of Daphne, Ovid wrote of Baucis and Philemon, whose love for each other was so great that, when they died, they were turned into an oak tree and a linden tree that grew side by side; Cyparissus, whom Apollo turned into a cypress tree so that the youth could forever mourn his accidental killing of his pet stag; Myrrha, who unwittingly slept with her father and prayed to the gods to be transformed into a myrrh tree to escape his wrath; and Hyacinthus, from whose blood a hyacinth flower sprang after his death.

Plants as manifestations of gods

Sometimes, plants are not just associated with gods and goddesses; they are actually worshiped as manifestations of deities—in other words, the form a deity assumes on earth. One example of this is tulsi, a type of basil plant, which Hindus identify with the goddess Tulasi. The plant is also closely associated with Vishnu. Vishnu, the preserver, is a member of the *trimurti* (trinity) of great Hindu gods, alongside Brahma, the creator, and Siva, the destroyer. According to myth, Vishnu seduced a beautiful woman named Vrinda by assuming the form of her husband Jalandhar, who died as a result of his wife's innocent infidelity. In one version of the story, when Vrinda discovered Vishnu's trickery, she cursed him and turned him into a stone; in return, the god transformed her into a tulsi plant. In another version, Vrinda threw herself onto her husband's funeral pyre and died, only to be reincarnated by Vishnu as tulsi. In both versions, Vrinda then became the goddess Tulasi, whose earthly manifestation was the tulsi plant. Many Hindus use the plant in rituals to worship Vishnu. However, some people worship tulsi itself. During British colonial rule in India in the 19th century, a census in British India's northwestern province recorded that 1,100 people described themselves not as Hindus, Muslims, or Sikhs, but simply as worshipers of the tulsi plant.

In Hindu mythology, the tulsi plant is also regarded as the meeting point between heaven and earth. Brahma lives on the plant's branches, other deities live on its leaves, and the sacred Ganges River lies at its roots. A number of

Below: This ivory statuette by Jean-Antoine Belleteste (1721–1811) depicts the nymph Daphne being transformed into a laurel tree while being pursued by Apollo.

1125

other cultures have also regarded sacred trees as a place where heaven and earth meet. Such trees were often believed to be the axis of the world. Norse peoples believed in a mythical tree called Yggdrasil, which linked a number of worlds, including Asgard, the home of the gods, Niflheim, the underworld, and Jotunheim, the land of the giants. The Norse believed that the world would come to an end after the apocalyptic battle of Ragnarok, but that two humans, Líf and Leifthrasir, would survive by seeking shelter in Yggdrasil. From their descendants would emerge a new race of people.

The Kikuyu of Kenya also believed that a sacred tree linked earth and heaven. One Kikuyu ritual involved a procession around a chosen tree, during which people spilled offerings of beer or milk on its trunk before sacrificing a lamb. The lamb was roasted and then eaten, although the Kikuyu set part of it aside as a sacrifice to their supreme god, Ngai. They placed this part of the lamb in the earth, to make the soil fertile and ensure rain. A variety of different trees have been associated with fertility, the exact species varying from culture to culture (see box, below).

Certain trees were also sacred to the ancient Greeks. One of the best-known examples was the oak tree at the oracle of Dodona in Epirus, northwest Greece. Priests and priestesses at the oracle observed the rustling of the tree's leaves in the breeze. They interpreted this noise as the voice of Zeus, king of the Olympian gods. In his epic the *Odyssey*, Greek poet Homer (c. ninth–eighth century BCE) described how the hero Odysseus went to Dodona to hear Zeus's message from the god's "high-crested oak." In another myth, the hero Jason's ship the *Argo* contained a timber from the Dodona oak in its prow. This timber allowed Zeus to make his will known by steering the ship in the direction he wanted.

Plants with magical powers

In many ancient cultures certain plants were believed to have magical properties. Some plants, such as the lotus flower, were widely associated with fertility. Others, such as hazel, could offer protection from bad magic or evil. The religious importance of plants was often closely connected with their physical characteristics: their size, shape, color, or smell, as well as the time of year they blossomed.

Many peoples throughout Europe and western Asia regarded the mandrake as sacred because its root was seen to look similar to a human body. The forked root was held to resemble two legs; in addition, a smaller root was believed to resemble male genitals. The humanlike qualities of the mandrake are reflected in the names people have given to it: the Romans called it *semihominus* (semihuman), the Greeks *anthropomorphon* (human-shaped), and the Turks *Adam-kökü* (human root). In many cultures, the mandrake was believed to bring fertility to barren women and to act as an aphrodisiac—indeed, another name for the Greek love goddess Aphrodite was Mandragoritis ("She of the Mandrake").

Sacred Trees of Life

Trees have traditionally played an important role in many cultures' beliefs. The baobab was worshiped in west Africa for its ability to bestow fertility on barren women. In the Limpopo Valley in southeast Africa rock drawings in a cave depict women with baobab seedpods instead of breasts, suggesting the tree's life-giving qualities. These qualities have been attributed in part to the girth of the baobab's trunk, which can be more than 100 feet (30 m) in circumference. In contrast, the life-giving potential of the banyan tree results from its milky sap. A myth of the Khond of Orissa, in northeast India, tells how the creator deity Nirantali told the banyan tree to feed the first humans with her milk. The banyan tree denied having any milk in its body, whereupon Nirantali struck it with an ax, causing milk to flow. The people drank the milk and survived until the first harvests came.

Left: In some African cultures baobab trees, such as this example found in Zimbabwe, were believed to be able to cure infertility.

The Mandrake and Fertility

The mandrake had a powerful impact on the imaginations of many ancient peoples. Folk beliefs from a number of countries relate how famous people owed their success to the possession of a mandrake: they included Macedonian empire-builder Alexander the Great (356–323 BCE) and French heroine and military leader Joan of Arc (c. 1412–1431). An ancient Greek legend tells the story of King Hermanos, who had no children because he was not inclined toward women. The king's sage, or wise man, advised him to obtain a mandrake and put some of his semen in it. The advice was good: Hermanos gained a son, whom he named Salaman. The mandrake also appears in Genesis, the first book of the Bible. Jacob's wife, Rachel, was unable to conceive until she begged her fertile sister, Leah, to give her some mandrake that had been found growing in a wheat field. Soon after obtaining the plant, Rachel became pregnant. The text in Genesis attributes Rachel's conception to God's will, but some scholars think that the story derives from a pre-biblical account, in which the mandrake was the source of fertility.

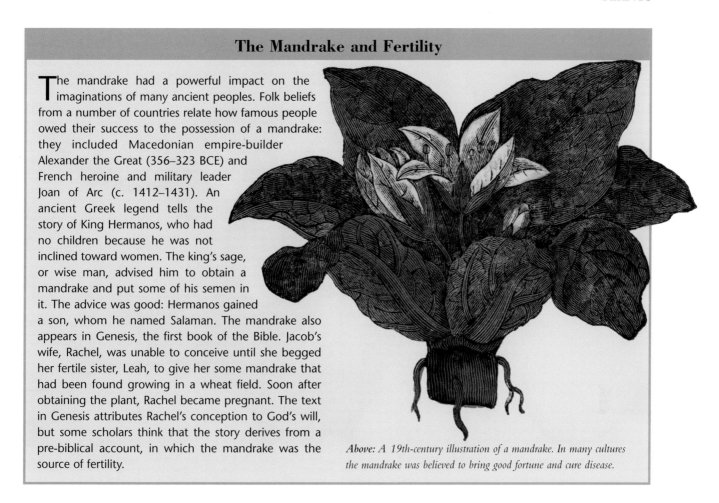

Above: A 19th-century illustration of a mandrake. In many cultures the mandrake was believed to bring good fortune and cure disease.

The mandrake had other life-enhancing qualities, too. Germanic peoples worshiped the plant as a familiar spirit, one that brought good luck and wealth to households. A Greek text written between the first and the third century CE records that mandrake was used as a cure for diseases and offered protection against grief, ruin, and all other types of misfortune (see box, above).

However, while the mandrake could bring fertility and good fortune, people also believed that it could bring harm. The fear surrounding this powerful plant is demonstrated by the elaborate procedures people went through when digging it up. Greek philosopher Theophrastus (c. 372–c. 287 BCE) described how mandrake collectors would draw three circles around the plant with a sword before digging. They would then enlist the help of an assistant, who would dance around the plant, speaking about the mysteries of love. Scholars believe that the three circles were intended to prevent the power of the plant from escaping, while the chanting about love may have been done to ensure the plant contained positive, aphrodisiac qualities. Theophrastus added that these procedures were necessary to prevent the mandrake from causing the collector harm.

There are strong parallels between the status of the mandrake in Europe and western Asia and that of ginseng in China. The Chinese also believe the ginseng root resembles a human being—one name for the plant is *jen-shen* (man-root). Like the mandrake, ginseng is regarded as containing supernatural, life-giving powers.

Good and evil properties

While it was the mandrake's physical appearance that earned it mythical importance, other plants gained their status because of their smell. Garlic and onions, for example, have been widely linked to evil forces. One west Asian myth recounts that garlic and onions sprang up from the left and right footprints left by Satan when he walked upon the earth. Furthermore, an Indian myth tells how garlic grew from the blood of a demon killed by Vishnu. The fact that these bulbs have to be pulled up from under the ground connected them with the underworld, strengthening their association with death and danger.

However, although garlic and onions were widely connected with evil, they could be used for positive purposes as well. For example, they could be used to placate or eliminate evil spirits. One Hittite myth tells

of a man who rid both himself and a god of evil by peeling an onion. Roman poet Persius (34–62 CE) told of people who ate garlic to ward off disease-carrying demons. The potential of garlic to be used for good or evil purposes is also indicated by the offerings of the plant that the ancient Greeks made to Hecate, the goddess of sorcery. Hecate had the ability both to bring and to cure disease and misery. The reputation of garlic's ability to ward off evil lives on today in countless horror films in which people use garlic to protect themselves from vampires.

Deadly nightshade

Many plants that are poisonous have been assumed to have magical properties. One of the most famous is deadly nightshade, which occurs throughout much of Europe. Eating the plant can have fatal consequences. However, if it is taken in minute quantities, it can have a hallucinogenic effect, the source of the widespread belief that people who took it could foresee the future. The plant has been widely associated with witchcraft—it was believed that witches rubbed themselves with the plant in order to gain the ability to fly.

Deadly nightshade's Latin name is *Atropa belladonna*. The first half of this name is derived from that of Atropos, one of the three Fates in Greek mythology. Atropos cut the

Above: Cloves of garlic, such as those pictured here, have long been believed to have magical properties..

thread that represented each human being's life. The derivation is a reflection of the plant's lethal nature. There are various explanations for the *belladonna* part of the name, which means "beautiful woman" in Italian. One is that people once believed that the plant could transform itself into the shape of a seductive enchantress upon whom it was dangerous to look. Other scholars have suggested that the name is taken from that of Bellona, the Roman goddess of war, whose priests may have drunk potions derived from the plant. However, it is most likely that it got its name from the hazardous practice among Italian women using the plant to dilate their pupils, believing this made them more beautiful.

ANDREW CAMPBELL

Bibliography

Lehner, Ernst, and Johanna Lehner. *Folklore and Symbolism of Flowers, Plants and Trees.* London: Marshall Cavendish, 1995.
Simoons, Frederick J. *Plants of Life, Plants of Death.* Mineola, NY: Dover Publications, 2003.

SEE ALSO: Apollo; Daphne; Demeter; Dionysus, Fertility; Hecate; India; Líf and Leifthrasir; Nature Religions; Osiris.

PLEIADES

In Greek mythology the Pleiades were the seven daughters of the Titan Atlas and the oceanid Pleione. According to legend, the sisters were immortalized by Zeus as a cluster of stars. One version said their half sisters made up the Hyades group of stars.

The Pleiades are a Y-shaped group of seven stars that are part of the constellation Taurus (the Bull). They are best seen in dark skies and are often almost invisible in cities because of light pollution. In the northern and southern hemispheres, the Pleiades, also known as the Seven Sisters, are located above Orion.

Although the names of the female characters involved in the Pleiades myth changed over time, the male characters generally remained the same. In one version of the myth the giant Orion, who was a hunter, became infatuated with

the seven sisters and pursued them relentlessly. According to Greek mythographer Apollodorus (fl.140 BCE), the sisters were walking in Boeotia (a region of Greece) with their mother when the hunter spotted by them. He pursued all the Pleiades until the gods decided to intervene. In some of the very early versions of the myth, it was Pleione rather than her daughters who was chased by Orion.

Zeus, the king of the gods, first turned the Pleiades into rock doves and then into stars. Some ancient authors wrote that the transformation of the women into stars began with their grief at Zeus's punishment of their father—Atlas was forced to carry the weight of the sky on his shoulders.

One story included the Hyades—five half sisters and a half brother, Hyas. Hyas died after being bitten by a snake, and the Hyades died of grief for him. The Pleiades died from mourning their half sisters. Out of pity, Zeus transformed them all—Hyades and Pleiades—into stars.

Below: The Pleiades are part of a larger cluster made up by hundreds of thousands of stars. The seven stars that constitute the Pleiades are the brightest of all of these stars..

The Pleiades in Literature

Mention of the Pleiades as stars appeared much earlier than details of the myth. The cluster is mentioned in the epics of Greek poet Homer (c. ninth–eighth century BCE), the *Iliad* and the *Odyssey*, and in the epic *Works and Days* by Greek poet Hesiod (fl. 800 BCE). Hesiod also called the grouping of stars the Atlageneis and said that their appearance signaled the beginning of the harvest.

The first text to give the individual stars names was a mere fragment of a poem that probably dates from the time of Hesiod. The individual stars were called Taygete, Electra, Alcyone, Sterope (or Asterope), Celaeno, Maia, and Merope. As a group they were called the Pleiades by the mythical singer Musaeus who quoted the poem and said that they were the daughters of Atlas.

Daughters of Pleione

In Greek myths, similar collective names were often given to members of a family. The ending *-ides* means "daughter of" and was added to the name of either the father (which was more common) or the mother. Thus in ancient Greek the daughters of Atlas would usually be called the Atlantides. There was, in fact, another group of minor goddesses by this name who appeared later in Greek mythology. They are said to be the daughters of Atlas and Hesperia and are sometimes called the Hesperides. Ancient collectors of myths explained the name Pleiades as meaning "daughters of Pleione."

In other versions a different goddess and even a mortal woman have been identified as the mother of the Pleiades.

Aethra, also a daughter of Oceanus, was called mother of the Pleiades in one source. Greek poet and scholar Callimachus (c. 305–c. 240 BCE) suggested that the Pleiades were daughters of an unnamed queen of the Amazons. He listed their names as Coccymo, Plaucia, Protis, Parthenia, Maia, Stonychia, and Lampatho. He also credited them with introducing nighttime festivals and choral dances to Greece. Later on, other authors felt free to list different goddesses as members of the Pleiades and to change details of the story. The names Dione, Asteria, and Calypso were included in the names of Pleiades at one time or another. The commonly accepted names are Maia, Electra, Taygete, Alcyone, Celaeno, Sterope, and Merope.

Lovers, husbands, and children

Although one version of the myth claimed that the Pleiades fled Orion because they were followers of the goddess Artemis (the virgin huntress) and had vowed to remain unmarried, most versions gave them husbands or lovers. Sterope (sometimes called Asterope) married Oenomaus, a son of the war god Ares and king of the Greek city of Pisa in Elis. Oenomaus and Sterope had a son named Leucippus and two daughters, Hippodameia and Alcippe. Leucippus was killed when he fell in love with a nymph named Daphne, who was a follower of Artemis. He disguised himself as female to be near her and was killed by the other nymphs when they discovered that he was actually a man.

Below: Remains of the ruined ancient city of Troezen still stand in Greece. According to mythology the city was built by Anthas and Hyperes, sons of the deity Poseidon and the Pleiad Alcyone.

Above: Two of the Pleiades are depicted descending from the sky in this 19th-century painting by English artist Henry Howard (1769–1847).

Hippodameia became famous for her beauty and was widely sought after, not only because of her looks but also because she was the heiress to the throne of Pisa. After Leucippus's death, whoever married Hippodameia would become king. Her father did not want her to marry, since an oracle had foretold that he would die by the hand of his daughter's husband. Oenomaus killed many of Hippodameia's suitors in chariot races until the hero Pelops rigged the race and killed the king.

Merope is the dimmest of all the Pleiades. The ancient Greeks explained this as being caused by her embarrassment because she was the only sister to marry a mortal. She married Sisyphus, son of Aeolus. When Sisyphus lay dying, he asked Merope not to bury him. When he got to Hades, however, he complained that his wife had neglected to bury him and asked for permission to return so that he could punish her. Once back among the living, he refused to return and was forcibly carried back to the underworld by the messenger god Hermes. There he was punished for this and other crimes by being set the endless task of rolling a huge stone to the top of a hill, only to have it roll back down each time.

Celaeno was the mother of two sons, Lycus and Chimareus, by either the sea god Poseidon or the Titan Prometheus. Alcyone, who was also called a lover of Poseidon, had several children by the god: one daughter, Aethusa, and four sons, Hyrieus, Hyperenor, Hyperes, and Anthas. Hyrieus is regarded as the founder of the royal dynasty at Thebes (a city in Boeotia), and Hyperes and Anthas built twin cities that would later unite to become the more famous city of Troezen (in southeast Greece).

Taygete, Maia, and Electra all had affairs with Zeus and had children by him. Taygete was reluctant at first and fled Zeus. The goddess Artemis attempted to help her by turning her into a cow (or a deer), but Zeus made love to her anyway—we are not told whether it was in animal form or not. In gratitude, Taygete gave Artemis the Ceryneian Hind, a deer with golden antlers. Heracles would later capture this deer as one of his labors. Taygete's son was Lacedaemon, mythical ancestor of the Spartans. He ruled a region that was named after him.

Maia gave birth to the god Hermes after Zeus visited her in a cave in Arcadia (in southern Greece). Electra had two sons by Zeus, Dardanus and Iasion, and became the ancestor of the Trojan royal house. One version said that when Troy fell, she left her sister stars and became a comet, although there is no evidence that this myth reflected an actual astronomical event.

LYN GREEN

Bibliography
Bulfinch, Thomas. *Bulfinch's Mythology.* New York: Modern Library, 1998.
Hesiod, and M. L. West, trans. *Theogony; and Works and Days.* New York: Oxford University Press, 1999.
Homer, and Robert Fagles, trans. *The Iliad.* New York: Penguin USA, 2003.

SEE ALSO: Ares; Artemis; Atlas; Calypso; Daphne; Heracles; Hermes; Hesperides; Oceanus; Orion; Pelops; Poseidon; Zeus.

PLUTUS

In ancient Greek mythology, Plutus was the god of abundance or wealth and the personification of riches (Greek: *ploutos*). He is sometimes confused with Pluton, another name for Hades, god of the dead.

According to Greek epic poet Hesiod (fl. 800 BCE), Plutus was born in Crete, the son of Demeter, goddess of fruitfulness, and Iasion, a mortal son of Zeus who was later killed by the king of the gods. The symbolism of this union seems to represent a "sacred marriage" between deity and mortal, making the earth fertile. In art, Plutus is sometimes represented as a child with a cornucopia, a horn filled to overflowing with fruits of the earth. While Plutus principally symbolized the riches of agricultural produce, by extension he became the god of every form of wealth. Proverbially in Greece, wealth was blind, and that is how the god first appears in the play *Plutus*, a comedy by Aristophanes (c. 450–c. 388 BCE). He soon recovers his sight, however, and sets about enriching only those who deserve him.

There was no religious cult of Plutus, but the child Plutus played a part in the Eleusinian Mysteries, where he was represented with Demeter and Persephone at the moment of their reunion, the time when fertility returned to the earth.

What's in a name

The similarity of the names Plutus and Pluton is unlikely to be accidental. The god of the dead was also sometimes depicted with a cornucopia. Many people regarded him as a giver of wealth because wealth comes from the earth, and it is to the earth that all mortals return when they die. Connected with this notion is the idea that humans have to be reconciled with the dead in order to prosper. The dead must be at peace for new life to go forward, and this idea is extended to the god of the dead. The Greeks propitiated their dead by giving them *meiligmata*, "soothing offerings." Pluton was sometimes known as Meilichios, meaning "soothed" or "soothing." Ancient Greeks sacrificed to Meilichios in the hope of having their luck improve, thus restoring prosperity and ending poverty and deprivation. The link between wealth and death was maintained in the art and literature of the Christian period. In *Paradise Lost*, English poet John Milton (1608–1674) remarks: "Let none admire [wonder] that riches grow in hell: that soil may best deserve the precious bane [poison]."

JAMES M. REDFIELD

Above: Plutus not only bestowed wealth, he also protected it. This bas-relief depicts him repelling scavenging birds from a vineyard.

Bibliography

Hesiod, and M. L. West, trans. *Theogony; and Works and Days*. New York: Oxford University Press, 1999.
Howatson, M. C., and Ian Chilvers. *Concise Oxford Companion to Classical Literature*. New York: Oxford University Press, 1993.

SEE ALSO: Demeter; Hades; Mystery Cults; Persephone.

POLYTHEISM

Polytheism is belief in many gods. Except for Judaism, Christianity, and Islam—monotheistic religions that share a common tradition of belief in one god—nearly all the world's other religions are polytheistic.

In polytheistic religious traditions most deities have particular powers and responsibilities. Some are general—nearly all such cultures have gods of thunder, love, and war, for example. Others are local and specific—they may guard the interests of a particular group or place. In Celtic Ireland, the old gods—known as "the people of the Sidhe"—were thought to be living parallel lives to their mortal worshipers. They were divided into three categories: learned gods, including druids, poets, and craftsmen; warriors and kings; and servant deities. Their duties and relationships with each other thus mirrored those of their human equivalents—some Irish gods were heroes, but most were menials. Among the numerous city deities of polytheism were Athena of Athens, Greece; Marduk of Babylon (part of modern Iraq); and Ptah of Memphis, Egypt. On a smaller scale, ancient Romans had a goddess of the domestic hearth, Vesta, and Penates, minor household divinities who were charged with taking care of the pantry.

Supreme but not perfect

Polytheism's multiplicity of deities is in contrast to the strictly monotheistic faiths in which the one god is all-powerful and all-knowing. The solitary deity is jealous and exclusive, so will not allow any rivals. As God tells Moses in the Old Testament of the Judeo-Christian Bible: "I am the Lord your God. You shall have no other gods beside Me." Some polytheistic religions have a supreme deity—examples include Egyptian Re, Hindu Siva, Norse Odin, and Greek Zeus—but he is neither omnipotent nor infallible. Zeus is dominant but not always victorious in his struggles with other deities. He is also capable of bad behavior, especially infidelity to his wife, Hera. Odin is similarly flawed: he does little that can be regarded as exemplary or

Left: Zeus, the chief of the Greek pantheon. This bust is by Phidias (fl. c. 490–430 BCE).

1133

Partial Family Tree of Ancient Greek Deities

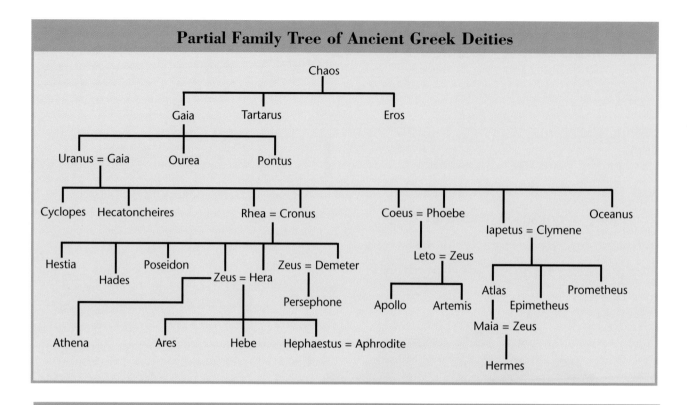

Hindu Polytheism

The Hindu religion has two great theistic movements: Vaishnavism, the cult of Vishnu, and Saivism, the cult of Siva. Hindu belief, however, usually holds that the universe is populated by a multitude of gods. These gods all display at least some features of the supreme being, or Godhead, and provide a link between the worshiper and the ultimate object of veneration. Yet for all their divinity, these gods also behave like humans—they may do good, but they may also display lust, greed, and spite. This view of the pantheon is similar to that of the ancient Greeks.

Supreme gods Brahma, Vishnu, and Siva and some of the other male gods are often able to fulfill their divine obligations only through relationships with female deities. These female consorts to the deities are known as Shakti. Other well-known gods are relatives of a supreme god, such as Ganesa, the elephant-headed god, a son of Siva and Parvati. Kali, or Durga, the consort of Siva, is worshiped widely throughout India in the autumn. Hanuman, the monkey-faced god, is depicted in many shrines, and along with Lakshmi, Vishnu's wife, is among the most important deities associated with Vaishnavism.

Above: Based on the popular Hindu epic Ramayana, *this 19th-century painting depicts the Hindu god Hanuman (seated).*

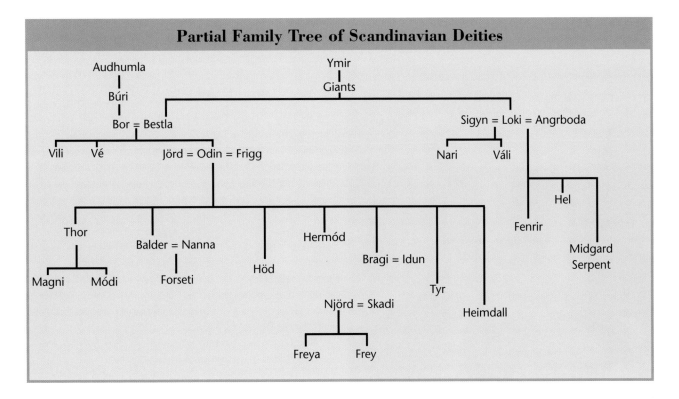

Partial Family Tree of Scandinavian Deities

moral in conventional human terms, and many of his famous exploits involve deception and extreme violence. For the Biblical God, such conduct would be an impossible contradiction: God is good by definition. When monotheists pray, they do so in the hope that God will answer their prayers, and in the belief that He is the sole judge of their case. If their desires conflict with those of their coreligionists, God will deliver the final verdict in the matter. In polytheism, believers invoke one particular god; if their chosen deity is less powerful than that of their adversary, their prayers will not be answered. In many polytheistic traditions all the gods and goddesses are members of a single family (see boxes, above and above left), and their relationships are explained in myths that reflect some aspect of reality. Much of the art and literature produced in polytheistic cultures use divine exploits to explain natural phenomena and illustrate human psychology. In ancient Egypt, the sun in the sky was believed to be the stately passage of Osiris in a flying ship. In *Prometheus Bound* by Aeschylus (525–456 BCE), the Greek playwright is widely thought to have used the story of the Titan's rebellion against the Olympian gods as a metaphor for the talented artist's rejection of the conventional values of society.

Some polytheistic religions have a supreme creator and focus of devotion. Hinduism, for example, has innumerable deities—estimates of the total number vary between 6 million and 33 million—but many believers regard them all as aspects of one supreme being (see box, opposite). Buddhists have gods but regard them as less important than the ultimate goal of human enlightenment. In addition to gods, many polytheistic cultures include belief in demonic and ghostly forces, some of which are malevolent. This is reflected to some extent in Christianity, but there is an important difference—the evil spirits in the New Testament are not gods.

Gods for all occasions

Polytheism is imaginative and flexible: it permits believers to worship many gods or a single god at certain times and for particular reasons. Ancient Romans, for example, might invoke Mercury to protect them on a journey or Cupid to help them woo a loved one. Such deities expect to be invoked only when there is something for them to do. The worship of one god does not preclude and is not prejudicial to the worship of another. This is quite different from the role of church saints: a Christian might pray to Saint Christopher or Saint Valentine (the patron saints of travelers and lovers, respectively), but the saints do not take action personally on the supplicant's behalf; they merely intercede with the monotheistic God—in this, as in all things, the decision would be His alone.

Polytheism may contain some of the elements of animism—the belief that everything in the world has its own consciousness—but is not in itself animistic. An animist might believe in the spirit of fire, but polytheistic

One God, Different Aspects

In polytheistic religious traditions, a single deity could have several different aspects, depending on location and circumstance. The worship of many Greek gods was panhellenic (all over Greece), but their significance differed from place to place. Apollo, for example, was worshiped principally in his native Delos, an island of the Cyclades in the Aegean Sea, and at Delphi on the southern slopes of Mount Parnassus, where he grew up. The two great sanctuaries in these places had little contact with each other and operated independently. In fact, Delian Apollo and Pythian (that is, Delphic) Apollo were effectively two separate gods, linked only by name. Many cities had sanctuaries dedicated to one Apollo or the other, and sometimes both, side by side. These sanctuaries might send ritual delegations to Delphi or Delos. Other sanctuaries of Apollo, however, maintained no connection with either Delos or Delphi.

Since there was no holy scripture of Greek religion, the powers and responsibilities of the deities were determined locally and sometimes seemed mutually contradictory. In some legends, Apollo was the bringer of plague; in others, he cured it. Nevertheless Apollo did have certain constant features in every account: he was always young, and always son of Zeus; he was always master of music, although his instrument was not always the lyre. The Muses he led were the children of Zeus, and the oracles he gave were the will of his father. Above all he was always Greek: the Romans generally assimilated Greek gods—they took Zeus, for example, to be no more than the Greek name of their own Jupiter—but they had no equivalent for Apollo, and they adopted him as he was from the Greek.

Left: The ruins of a classical building stand on the Greek island of Delos, traditionally the birthplace of Apollo.

fire deities such as Roman Vulcan and Hindu Agni are personified beings—they have human or humanlike characteristics—whereas in animism fire is simply a force of nature. Polytheistic gods are used in art and literature to represent various aspects of human behavior and psychology: Mars bellicosity; Bacchus drunkenness; Nemesis revenge. In animism no such transformations are imagined.

Types of god

While it is difficult to generalize about polytheism worldwide, it is possible to discern certain broad tendencies. Most religions of this type have three main categories of divinities: sky gods, atmospheric gods, and earth deities. In Hinduism, the three types are clearly differentiated: Surya is the sun god; Indra is responsible for storms and rain; Agni is the god of earth and fire. In Greek polytheism, many of the gods are extensively adaptable: Zeus is primarily a sky god, but he also causes thunder and lightning. The spectacular auditory and visual effects caused by these natural phenomena made it only a small imaginative step to turn sky gods into gods of war. Some deities formed unions that symbolized the link between earth and sky. Examples include the marriages of Abzu and Tiamat in Mesopotamia, Siva and Sakti in India, and Gaia and Uranus in Greece. Matters are further complicated by the interchangeability of the roles of many gods. Greeks hoping to win a battle or a game might sacrifice to Athena, goddess of war, but they might equally make offerings to Nike, goddess of victory. Sometimes the more important deity would assimilate the lesser one. Thus Athena was sometimes known as Athena Nike; Zeus, when called on to punish perjury, was known as Zeus Horkios ("of oaths"). Any supplementary identifying term such as these was known as an *epiklesis* ("extra name").

Other sky deities

The outstanding power and prestige of most sun gods—Helios in Greece, Mithras in Persia, Re in Egypt—are widely taken as indications that early humans recognized that the sun was the source of all life on earth, and the only force strong enough to conquer darkness. Light and life were mutually dependent and inextricable. In general, the moon was less important in polytheistic mythology, and was often an ambivalent figure—this has been taken to symbolize the uncertainty of early civilizations about the satellite's purpose. Yet even that is not always the case. At Ur, the ancient city of Babylon, for example, the supreme deity was Sin, a moon god. Known as Nanna by Sumerians, Sin was the "lamp of heaven and earth," "lord of the months," and "lord of decisions." His consort was Ningal, and their children were mother goddess Ishtar and sun god Shamash.

Many polytheistic religions also embraced elements of astrology, an attempt to make the planets and stars significant to daily life on earth. Astrology became important to Buddhists and Hindus in Asia, and in the theology of the Aztecs and especially the Maya of Central America. It was also significant in Europe and in the Arab world until it was sidelined by monotheistic Christianity and Islam. Astrology is still practiced, of course, and influences the conduct of many people, but in monotheistic societies it is not taken seriously and its status is reduced to that of a superstitious parlor game.

Above: This sculpture of the second century BCE depicts the Greek goddess of wisdom, crafts, and war in her manifestation as Athena Nike, goddess of victory.

Cults

Unlike monotheistic religions, polytheism does not generally concern itself with human salvation. Among the exceptions to this general rule in Greece were the mystery cults, which offered purification from sin and a better life after death by performing ecstatic rites. The most notable ancient religions of this type were those that venerated Dionysus or Demeter and her daughter Persephone. Later, during the Hellenistic period—Greco-Roman civilization between the death of Alexander the Great in 323 BCE and the beginning of the Roman Empire in 30 BCE—salvation cults of certain Asian gods became widespread throughout the Greek and Roman world. The most important of these were the cults of Mithras (from Syria), Cybele (from Anatolia, a region of modern Turkey), and Serapis, Isis, and Osiris (from Egypt). These cults promised something that polytheism almost never offered—a better life. Such gods inspired a degree of fervor unusual in polytheism and provided part of the cultural context for the spread of Christianity. These gods of salvation, however, did not require exclusive devotion; like most polytheistic deities, they were not jealous—as Greek philosopher Plato (c. 428–c. 348 BCE) had put it: "Envy stands outside the divine chorus." There are numerous accounts in which deities help each other: Apollo advises on how to deal with Serapis and Mithras; Osiris orders sacrifices to Zeus.

Fertility deities

Many ancient polytheistic religions worshiped gods of fertility above all other deities. Within this category are earth mothers—goddesses who either created the earth or gave birth to it—and agricultural deities such as Babylonian Ishtar, Egyptian Osiris, Greek Demeter, Mesopotamian Tammuz, and Phrygian Attis. Sacred significance was often attached to topographical features. Mountains, such as Olympus in Greece, had resident deities; rivers, such as the Ganges, were also the homes of gods and goddesses. Underground rivers had special significance because they linked the surface of the earth with the underworld. Some places had cosmic significance—Delphi, Greece, was known as the navel (omphalos) of the earth. Further, many cultures had gods and goddesses associated with the sea—examples include Greek Poseidon and Norse Aegir.

In several polytheistic cultures, trees and plants have been deified. This is sometimes because they represent a link between heaven and earth—they have their roots in the ground and their highest branches in the sky. Oaks, for example, are thought to have been venerated by druids. In other cases, a specific plant is regarded as a special source

Below: Polytheistic religions often adopted the deities of other cultures. This Roman fresco shows a religious ceremony in honor of Isis, suggesting that the Egyptian goddess was also worshiped in Italy.

Above: *The goddess Bendis was imported from Thrace in northeast Greece and assimilated into the Athenian pantheon as a manifestation of Artemis, goddess of hunting.*

Yaksas

In the mythology of India, yaksas are largely benevolent nature spirits who protect hidden treasures, especially those buried in the roots of trees. Unlike Greek dryads, whose sphere of influence was restricted to trees, yaksas are often worshiped as guardian deities of cities, districts, lakes, or wells.

The leading yaksa is Kubera—also known as Vaisravana and Jambhala—a god of wealth who rules a mythical Himalayan kingdom named Alaka from a palace on Mount Kailasa, where he lives in great luxury and is attended by innumerable genies. Kubera is a popular figure in art and literature, where he is usually depicted as a dwarfish figure with a large paunch, holding a money bag or a pomegranate and sometimes riding on the back of a male servant. In Buddhist sculptures he is often shown accompanied by a mongoose. Kubera is associated with, and has power over, the whole earth, especially its mountains, and all the treasures that lie within it—mainly minerals and jewels but also water.

According to some versions of the legend, Kubera came originally from Sri Lanka but was driven out of his native land by his half brother, Ravana. Ravana is the Hindu king of the demons (*raksasas*) who had 10 heads and 20 arms. He features prominently in the central incidents of the popular epic *Ramayana*. In other versions of the story, however, it was Kubera who forced Ravana out of his homeland.

of goodness or a symbol of divine power—examples include the vine in the Mediterranean region and maize in Central America. Sometimes trees are believed to contain spirits, such as the dryads of ancient Greece and the yaksas of India (see box, left).

Animal deities

In polytheism, many species of animals are divine. Snakes were important fertility symbols in India, perhaps because they lived in the earth, the source of all sustenance. They are nearly always wise. In the Babylonian *Epic of Gilgamesh* it is a serpent that knows the secret of rejuvenation. The feathered serpent Quetzalcoatl was the creator god of the Aztecs, while the Maya worshiped Kukulkan, a counterpart of Quetzalcoatl who taught them agriculture. Snakes, however, are demonized in monotheistic traditions, most notably in the Old Testament story in which a serpent persuades Eve, the first woman, to eat the forbidden fruit of the tree of knowledge. This leads to her expulsion, with her husband, Adam, from the Garden of Eden. In Aztec tradition, the gods Cipactli and Huitzlipochtli took the form of a hummingbird and an alligator, respectively. In Hindu religion, Nandi is a bull, while boar, fish, and

Polytheistic Revival

Some polytheistic religions have been displaced by monotheism: those of ancient Greece and Rome were superseded by Christianity, while Egyptian and Mesopotamian beliefs in many gods were eventually ousted by Islam. In some parts of Africa and Polynesia, Christianity and Islam have become established as the official state religions, but in many areas ancient beliefs and rituals still persist.

Elsewhere ancient polytheisms are still very much alive: Hinduism, for example, currently has more than 800 million followers in India. Another example is the Japanese Shinto religion, which is both polytheistic and animistic and continues to thrive. There are in addition a significant number of polytheistic religions of more recent foundation. Present-day religions of this type include Asatru (a modern Icelandic continuation of old Norse forms of worship) and Vodun (practiced by Yoruba people in Nigeria, Benin, and Togo). Buddhism is also sometimes described as a polytheistic religion, although this label is rejected by most believers. Similarly, some Jewish and Islamic scholars have suggested that the Christian doctrine of the Holy Trinity—God the Father, God the Son, and God the Holy Spirit—borders on polytheism, but Christians strongly deny that that is the case. However, even discounting these controversial cases, most religions are today, as throughout human history, polytheistic.

tortoise are among the many avatars (incarnations) of Vishnu. In ancient Celtic religion, Cernunnos was a stag god with antlers.

Deification

Humans can become polytheistic gods, too. Most commonly it was monarchs who were deified—Egyptian pharaohs, Chinese, Japanese, and Roman emperors— but nonroyals could be apotheosized (given divine status) if they were sufficiently important. Kuan Ti, a Chinese folk hero who robbed the rich to give money to the poor, like Robin Hood in medieval England, was captured and executed in 219 CE. His posthumous fame grew as rulers conferred successively greater titles upon him. Finally, in 1594 CE, he was apotheosized as god of war, protector of China and all its citizens. In Greco-Roman culture, some mythological heroes of mixed parentage—half human, half divine—became gods in the afterlife. Examples include Aeneas, son of the mortal Anchises and the goddess Aphrodite; and Heracles, whose mother, Alcmene, was one of many mortal women with whom Zeus committed adultery.

In polytheism, almost anything could have a god. There were gods who looked after particular areas of human endeavor, such as Asclepius, Greek god of medicine, and Kvasir, Norse god of poetry; there were gods of war, such as Mars in ancient Rome and Skanda in India; and gods of love, such as Aphrodite (Greece) and Kama (India). Even the points of the compass may have their own divinities. Some of the most powerful polytheistic gods were those that had the power of judgment of human souls after death, such as Osiris in Egypt, Yama in India, Hades in Greece, and Hel in Scandinavia.

JAMES M. REDFIELD

Left: This hardwood figurine from the 18th century CE comes from the Cook Islands and depicts a male Polynesian deity giving birth to subordinate gods from his chest.

Bibliography

Daniélou, Alain. *The Gods of India: Hindu Polytheism.* New York: Inner Traditions International, 1985.

Gardell, Mattias. *Gods of the Blood.* Durham, NC: Duke University Press, 2003.

Kirsch, Jonathan. *God against the Gods: The History of the War between Monotheism and Polytheism.* New York: Viking, 2004.

SEE ALSO: Ares; Athena; Demeter; Dionysus; Greece; India; Monotheism; Nature Religions; Persephone; Prehistoric Religion; Zeus.

POMONA

Pomona was the Roman goddess of fruit (*poma*), especially apples and pears. She was famous for her devotion to her orchards and for her chastity. The main story attached to her revolves around her eventual seduction by the nature god Vertumnus.

Above: This 19th-century tapestry by Edward Burne-Jones (1833–1898) and William Morris (1834–1896) depicts Pomona holding a branch from an apple tree.

The story of Pomona and Vertumnus is told by Roman poet Ovid (43 BCE–17 BCE) in his *Metamorphoses*. According to Ovid, Pomona dwelled in Latium in the days of King Proca and was more beautiful than any other woman who lived there. However, Pomona did not want to have anything to do with love. No faun or satyr could seduce her. Even the fertility god Priapus tried and failed. However, one nature god, Vertumnus, fell so madly in love with Pomona that he became determined to make her his wife.

The seduction of Pomona

Vertumnus was the Roman god of the changing seasons, and as such could take on any shape he wanted. He used this ability to spy on Pomona. Sometimes he turned into a farmer's son and, carrying a heavy basket on his shoulders, walked by the vegetable garden where Pomona worked. At other times he came to her orchard as a fruit farmer, a cattle herder, or a fisherman. In these various guises he watched the goddess as she tended to her orchard.

Eventually, in an attempt to win her hand, Vertumnus adopted a different disguise. Transforming himself into the shape of an old woman, he approached Pomona's garden. He first complimented her on the beauty of the apples that hung from the trees in her orchard, and then he told her that the most beautiful thing in the garden was Pomona herself. Vertumnus pointed to an elm tree around which a vine was attached. He explained to the nymph how the tree and the vine complemented one another and how the vine needed the tree to support it.

"And yet, Pomona," Vertumnus went on, "you haven't learned a thing from the lesson of the elm and the vine. You, who are so beautiful, will attach yourself to no-one. Worse, you run away from love, while all the people in your surroundings—gods, demigods, even mortals—are in love with you. Listen to me, an old woman who cares about you more than anyone. Choose a husband. And choose the best—Vertumnus."

Vertumnus went on to list the reasons why he would make such a good husband. From the safety of his disguise he gave Pomona a detailed description of Vertumnus's good looks and his ability to change shape at will. He went on to describe to Pomona the god's love of nature and gardens. Most important of all, he told the goddess about Vertumnus's undying and absolute love for her. Finally, he told her that she should beware the wrath of Venus, goddess of love. In order to illustrate the dangers of incurring the goddess's anger, Vertumnus told Pomona the story of Iphis and Anaxarete.

1141

Above: Vertumnus and Pomona, *by Dutch artist Adriaen van de Velde, is one of the most famous depictions of the pair's courtship.*

Iphis and Anaxarete

The son of a poor widow, Iphis fell in love with a rich and beautiful girl named Anaxarete. Day after day, he went to the gate of her home and begged the servants to give her his love letters. The staff did what he asked, but still Anaxarete would have nothing to do with him. At long last Iphis gave up. Unable to win her love, he tied a rope to the gate and hanged himself. Before he did so, however, he prayed to the gods that he would become famous because of his suffering.

A few days later the funeral procession took Iphis's body past the house of Anaxarete. This was the moment for Venus's revenge. Anaxarete, who heard the wailing and weeping outside her house, went to the window to look at the procession. However, when she saw the body of Iphis on the bier, her gaze froze. The blood drained from her body. She tried to walk away, but she could not—she stood riveted before the window. Anaxarete's body gradually turned to stone to match her heart.

Once he had completed his story, Vertumnus asked Pomona if her heart too was made of stone. He then threw off his disguise and revealed himself in his true form. Pomona, won over by his charm and eloquence, agreed to become his lover.

Historians know very little about Pomona other than the details preserved in the story recorded by Ovid. However, it is known that she had a sanctuary, the Pomonal, some 12 miles (19 km) outside Rome on the road to Ostia. Pomona had no holidays on the Roman calender and is therefore believed to have had only movable feasts, which could take place on various dates.

Pomona in art

There are no surviving representations of Pomona from ancient Greek or Roman art. In later art, however, Pomona is often depicted with Vertumnus. Among the best known representations of the pair are two paintings by 17th-century Dutch artists. Both works are entitled *Vertumnus and Pomona* and show Vertumnus courting the goddess while disguised as an old woman. One is by Adriaen van de Velde (1636–1672); the other is by Paulus Moreelse (1571–1638). Pomona is also depicted in a group sculpture by French artist Camille Claudel (1864–1943).

FEYO SCHUDDEBOOM

Bibliography

Bulfinch, Thomas. *Bulfinch's Mythology.* New York: Modern Library, 1998.
Ovid, and A. D. Melville, trans. *Metamorphoses.* New York: Oxford University Press, 1998.

SEE ALSO: Priapus; Rome.

POSEIDON

Poseidon was the Greek god of the sea. He was known for both his violent temper and his tendency to bear long grudges—the Greek hero Odysseus was just one mythical character to suffer because he had offended the god. Like his brother Zeus, Poseidon had a voracious sexual appetite and fathered a large number of children. Many of the myths attached to him revolve around the tragic consequences of his violent pursuit of mortals.

There are various theories about the origins of Poseidon. The god was worshiped as Poseidon Heliconius by the Ionians, a race of people who migrated from mainland Greece to western Asia around 1000 BCE. Some scholars have suggested that, if this name was derived from that of Mount Helicon in Boeotia, Poseidon might originally have been a sky god. Poseidon's characteristic trident, or three-pointed spear, could once have been a thunderbolt. The god's connection with bulls and horses, on the other hand, suggests an association with fertility. His name is probably derived from the Greek for "husband of Da," that is, flowing water. This would suggest that Poseidon was a version of a common Indo-European god associated with rivers and other water sources.

Whatever his origins, it is as the fearsome ruler of the seas that Poseidon is best known today. According to Greek poet Hesiod (fl. 800 BCE), Poseidon was one of the six children of the Titans Rhea and Cronus. When Poseidon and his siblings were born, their mother Rhea had to watch in horror as her husband ate their children. Cronus had heard a prophecy from his mother, the earth goddess Gaia, that one of his children would kill him. However, Rhea managed to save Zeus, her youngest child, by giving Cronus a stone to swallow in his place and hiding the boy in a cave on Crete. When Zeus grew up, he forced his father to vomit up all the divine children. Together, Zeus and his brothers Hades and Poseidon got their revenge on Cronus by driving him away and taking over his kingdom. Lots were drawn to determine who would take over the various parts of

Right: A depiction of Poseidon from a sixth-century-BCE Greek dish. Poseidon is carrying his most famous attribute, the trident.

God of Earthquakes

As well as being god of the sea, Poseidon was also the god of earthquakes. The Greek poet Homer (c. ninth–eighth century BCE) uses various titles to reflect this aspect of his personality. One of these titles is *Gaieochos*, which means "holder of the earth." This title reflects the idea that the sea encircled the earth, holding it in its place. Another epithet that Homer uses to describe him is *Enosichthon*, which means "earth shaker." Certain areas of Greece are badly afflicted by earthquakes, and in ancient times these regions were often home to Poseidon cults. One was the Isthmus of Corinth, where the Isthmian games were held every two years in honor of the god; another was Helice in Achaea. According to Greek geographer Strabo (c. 64 BCE–c. 23 CE), the city was devastated by an earthquake and a tidal wave in 373 BCE. Both were said to be the work of Poseidon.

Cronus's realm. Zeus became ruler of sky and earth, Hades of the underworld, and Poseidon of the sea.

Other authors offer alternative versions of Poseidon's parentage. One variation has Rhea putting a young horse in Poseidon's place, saving him from being swallowed, as she later saved Zeus. In this story Poseidon's association with horses goes back to the very earliest point in his life. Another myth says that Poseidon was thrown into the sea by his father and then went on to rule his watery habitat.

Poseidon and Amphitrite

Poseidon's wife was the sea nymph Amphitrite. According to one story, when Poseidon first courted her, Amphitrite fled from him. Poseidon sent all the sea creatures in pursuit of her. Eventually Delphinus, the dolphin, found her and pleaded on the god's behalf. Amphitrite was eventually won over by the dolphin's persuasive powers and agreed to marry the god. As a reward, Poseidon placed the dolphin in the sky as a constellation. Other accounts of the origins of the marriage show a darker side to the sea god's nature, saying that Poseidon carried the nymph off, raped her, and made her his wife against her will.

In ancient art Poseidon was depicted as handsome, bearded, and fierce, a figure very much like his brother Zeus. Like his brother, Poseidon was an unfaithful husband and betrayed his wife on numerous occasions. For example, he chased after Demeter while the grain goddess was searching the earth for her stolen daughter, Persephone. Demeter transformed herself into a mare, but Poseidon took the form of a stallion and raped the goddess. The

coupling produced both a daughter, Despoina, and a magical horse, Areion. Later Areion came into the possession of the Greek hero Heracles.

Many of the recipients of Poseidon's sexual attentions suffered greatly because of them. One was a beautiful young girl named Caenis, whose story is told by Roman poet Ovid (43 BCE–17 BCE) in his *Metamorphoses*, a collection of stories in which the main figures undergo some form of transformation. Poseidon raped the girl and then offered her any gift that she named. Caenis asked that she be turned into a man so that she should never endure such an ordeal again. Poseidon granted her wish, transforming her into a man named Caeneus, giving him the additional gift of invulnerability. Caeneus was later involved in the battle between the centaurs and the Lapiths, a people who lived in Thessaly. The battle occurred at a wedding feast, and Caeneus's gift of invulnerability enabled him to kill many of the centaurs. Eventually, however, they hammered him into the ground with tree trunks.

Another figure whose life was blighted by her sexual liaison with Poseidon was Medusa, a beautiful woman who made love to the sea god in Athena's temple. According to one version of Medusa's story, recorded by Greek writer Apollodorus (fl. 140 BCE), Athena was so incensed that she transformed Medusa into a hideous monster. The vain Medusa was particularly proud of her beautiful head of hair, so Athena turned it into a mass of writhing snakes. Medusa's head was so ghastly to see that all who set eyes on her were transformed into stone. Athena's persecution of Medusa did not end with the transformation, however. Much later she helped the Greek hero Perseus kill the monster.

Children of Poseidon

Poseidon and Amphitrite had several children, the most notable of whom was the sea god Triton, who was a man from the waist up and a fish from the waist down and who blew a horn made from a conch shell. By blowing this shell Triton was able to calm the seas. Triton also appears in the story of Jason and the Argonauts, swimming beside the *Argo* and leading the ship to safety. However, like his father, Triton had a darker side and was said to attack boats and rape women bathing in the sea.

Poseidon also had many children with other goddesses and women, most notably the earth goddess Gaia. One of the pair's most famous offspring was the giant Antaeus, who ruled over Libya. The Greek hero Heracles came to the country as part of his search for the garden of the

Above: This statue of Poseidon by Greek sculptor Calamis dates to the fifth century BCE. It was recovered off the coast of Greece in 1928.

Erechtheus

Erechtheus was a mythical hero and king of Athens. According to legend, he was the son of the earth goddess Gaia and was raised by the goddess Athena. Erechtheus defended the city of Athens against the Thracian king Eumolpus. This king was Poseidon's son and ancestor of the priests of Eleusis. Despite the patronage of his father, Eumolpus died at the hands of Erechtheus. In revenge, Poseidon drove Erechtheus into the earth with a blow of his trident.

Erechtheus is often confused with his father, Erichthonius, also a king of Athens. Both kings were often conflated with Poseidon and were worshiped at their own cult sites. The Athenians built a temple to Erechtheus, the Erechtheum, on the Acropolis. One of the temple's altars was jointly dedicated to both Erechtheus and Poseidon.

Below: In this woodcut, Greek hero Odysseus is depicted sailing between Scylla and Charybdis. Both sea monsters came into existence as a result of Poseidon's lustful behavior.

Hesperides, the location of the golden apples of immortality. Gaia had originally given the miraculous apple tree to Zeus and Hera at their marriage. Antaeus challenged everyone who came to his land to a wrestling match. He inevitably won the contests, and he used the skulls of his defeated opponents to decorate the temple of his father, Poseidon. The secret of Antaeus's success lay in the fact that whenever a part of his body touched the ground, he gained strength through contact with his mother, Gaia. However, Heracles overcame him by hoisting him into the air and crushing him until he perished.

Scylla and Charybdis

Another fearsome offspring of Gaia and Poseidon was Charybdis, a giantess who was cast into the ocean by Zeus. Charybdis was chained to the seabed. Three times each day she sucked the water above her downward, causing a giant whirlpool to appear on the ocean's surface. The whirlpool was so strong that any ship caught in it was certain to be destroyed. To make matters worse, Charybdis lived in the Straits of Messina, which separate Italy and Sicily. The other side of the straits was the home of the six-headed sea

Above: Perseus and Andromeda *by Rutilio Manetti (1571–1639).*
Andromeda sits chained while the sea monster sent by Poseidon approaches.

monster Scylla. Scylla lived in a cave halfway up a cliff and would reach down and seize sailors as their ships went past. All travelers who passed through the straits thus faced an unenviable choice. In order to give one of the monsters a wide berth, they would be forced to sail close to the other, putting themselves in mortal danger.

There are various stories that attempt to explain Scylla's origins. One of them says that Scylla was originally a beautiful maiden, the daughter of Crateis, usually identified with Hecate, the goddess of witchcraft. When Poseidon tried to court Scylla, Amphitrite flew into a rage. The betrayed wife was so furious that she threw a potion into Scylla's bath that turned the luckless maiden into a sea monster. This story makes Scylla another unfortunate victim of Poseidon's uncontrolled lust, just like Medusa and Caenis.

Either purposefully or unintentionally, Poseidon was responsible for most of the monsters who dwelled in the already dangerous waters of the sea. He could easily be offended and was capable of inflicting terrible punishments on mortals who slighted him. For example, Cassiopeia, queen of Ethiopia, once boasted that she was more beautiful than any of the Nereids, the sea nymphs who were daughters of another sea god, Nereus. The Nereids were so offended that they asked Poseidon to punish Cassiopeia. First, Poseidon sent a tidal wave that flooded

her land. Then he sent a sea monster to attack her people. When the queen and her husband, Cepheus, consulted an oracle to see how they could rid their land of its plight, they were told that they would have to sacrifice their daughter Andromeda to the sea beast. The king and queen tried to do so, chaining Andromeda to a rock, but the girl was saved at the last minute by the hero Perseus.

Poseidon and Odysseus

Once a mortal had offended Poseidon, he or she could not expect the crime to be either forgiven or forgotten. The sea god's most famous longstanding quarrel was with Odysseus. The Greek hero gained Poseidon's enmity by gouging out the eye of the god's son, the giant Cyclops Polyphemus. Odysseus and his men, on their way home from the Trojan War, had entered the giant's cave and stolen food from him. Polyphemus retaliated by shutting the hero and his crew in the cave with a great stone and proceeding to eat the sailors, one at a time. Odysseus craftily got Polyphemus drunk, then drove a wooden stake into the giant's single eye. Tricking Polyphemus by hiding under the giant's sheep as they passed through the cave door, Odysseus and his men sped away in their ship.

Above: This terra-cotta relief from the fourth century CE shows Amphitrite, wife of Poseidon, riding a sea monster.

Polyphemus roared out curses after them and begged his father, Poseidon, to grant him a favor. He begged that Odysseus should never make it back to his beloved homeland, or that, if he did, then he should do so without either his ship or his men, having suffered many torments on his travels. Poseidon granted Polyphemus's request and proved to be a persistent adversary for Odysseus, unleashing a series of violent storms that almost cost the hero his life. Odysseus managed to survive only with the help of another deity, the goddess Athena, who protected and guided him on his travels.

The rivalry of Poseidon and Athena

Poseidon and Athena were often adversaries in Greek mythology. Many years earlier, the two deities had vied for the position of divine ruler of Athens and Attica. The two deities demonstrated their powers by creating magical gifts for the Athenians. Poseidon struck a stone with his trident, and a saltwater spring erupted from the place where the trident hit the rock. Athena, meanwhile, touched the earth with her spear, and an olive tree grew. Cecrops, the king of Athens, judged that Athena's gift was more useful and built a temple to her on the Acropolis, the central hill in Athens. The king's decision drove Poseidon into a fury, and the sea god sent a flood to punish the Athenians. In order to appease the god, they built another temple, dedicated specifically to him, in the center of their city. The legend of the contest remained popular with Athenians for centuries. Greek travel writer Pausanias (143–176 CE) claimed that he was shown the mark where Poseidon's trident struck the rock.

Poseidon clashed with two other deities over the possession of regions. According to Pausanias, the sea god vied with Hera over the region of Argos. When the river gods Inachus, Cephissus, and Asterion ruled in favor of Hera, Poseidon once again flew into a rage. In spite, he dried up the three gods' rivers, causing the region to be barren. Poseidon also competed with the sun god Helios for the city of Corinth. In this case Helios was granted supremacy over the city itself, while Poseidon was allowed to rule the isthmus on which it was located.

As well as the sea, Poseidon was also associated with bulls and horses (see box, opposite). In two famous myths,

Poseidon Hippion—God of Horses

Even though he was the god of the sea, the animal with which Poseidon was most closely associated was the horse. He was sometimes known as Poseidon Hippion—*hippos* is the Greek work for the animal. There are many myths that associate Poseidon with horses. Roman poet Virgil (70–19 BCE) claimed that Poseidon created the first horse by striking the earth with his trident. A more famous equine creation of Poseidon was the winged horse Pegasus. The Gorgon Medusa was pregnant by Poseidon when she was beheaded by Greek hero Perseus. The pair's offspring—Pegasus—sprung fully formed from her neck. Poseidon also gave the immortal horses Xanthus and Balius to Peleus, the father of Greek hero Achilles.

Horses were often sacrificed to Poseidon. Greek writer Pausanias wrote that in the region of Argolis, horses were drowned in a river as an offering to the god.

Right: This Greek silver coin from the third century BCE depicts the winged horse Pegasus.

bulls sent by Poseidon from the sea were the cause of great tragedy. King Minos of Crete had prayed to the sea god to send him a fabulous bull, which he would immediately sacrifice. Poseidon sent a bull so beautiful Minos could not bear to give it up. He decided to use the bull to enrich his herd and sacrificed another in its place. Poseidon went into a rage. He caused Pasiphae, Minos's wife, to fall in love with the bull. Daedalus, the court artist, created the lifelike form of a cow for Pasiphae to hide in so that the creature could have intercourse with her. The offspring of their union was a monster, the Minotaur, that was a source of tragedy for many years.

Another bull sent from the sea by Poseidon brought tragedy to the life of Hippolytus, the son of Athenian hero Theseus. Theseus's wife, Phaedra, fell in love with her young stepson, and when he rejected her advances, she committed suicide, claiming that Hippolytus had tried to rape her. Theseus was so angry that he called on Poseidon to avenge him. The sea god promptly sent a bull from the sea to the beach where Hippolytus was driving his chariot. The bull so terrified Hippolytus's horses that he was thrown from his chariot and dragged to his death by his horses' reins.

The worship of Poseidon

The Greeks were a nation of seafarers and, as such, treated Poseidon with great reverence. The fact that his name appears frequently on Linear B tablets found at Mycenae shows that he was worshiped at a very early stage of Greek history. Linear B was a form of script that was used between 1400 and 1150 BCE. Classical sources show that Poseidon was also widely worshiped in later times. For example, in his *Guide to Greece*, Pausanias lists numerous temples that were dedicated to the god. Among the most notable were those at Athens, Argos, Sparta, and the islands of Tenís and Achaea. The finest example of a temple to Poseidon to still exist today is probably that at Sounion in Attica, a region of central Greece. The building was constructed sometime between 450 and 440 BCE and is made of marble. The partially destroyed frieze on one side of the building is believed to show a fight between Athena and Poseidon for control of Attica.

The most famous festival held in honor of Poseidon was the Isthmian Games. The games were held on the Isthmus of Corinth, which was believed to come under the divine

POSEIDON

Above: *The temple of Poseidon at Sounion, Greece. Built in the fifth century BCE, the building is the best preserved temple to the sea god to still exist.*

protection of the god. The Isthmian Games were first held in the sixth century BCE and consisted of athletic events as well as poetry and music contests. A number of sacrifices were made to Poseidon. Among the animals sacrificed were the two most closely associated with the sea god—horses and black bulls.

Poseidon in art

In Roman times, Poseidon came to be identified with the god Neptune. Both Poseidon and his Roman equivalent have been widely represented in art. One of the most famous ancient statues of Poseidon still to exist is by fifth-century-BCE sculptor Calamis. The statue was recovered from the sea off the coast of Artemisium in Greece in the early 20th century. It stands almost 7 feet (2.1 m) tall.

Since Calamis's day, there have been many sculptures of Poseidon and Neptune. The representations of the god invariably depict him as bearded and muscular and usually carrying his most famous attribute, the trident. Because of his association with water, statues of Poseidon are often found in fountains. Possibly the most famous of such statues is that found in the Trevi Fountain in Rome. It was created by Niccoló Salvi (1697–1751). It depicts the sea god in a chariot drawn by horses. Another famous statue is one by Italian sculptor Bartolommeo Ammannati (1511–1592). It stands in the Piazza della Signoria in the city of Florence, Italy.

The sea god has also been a popular subject for painters, Among the most famous paintings to depict Poseidon or Neptune are *Triumph of Neptune and Amphitrite* by Nicolas Poussin (1594–1665); *Jupiter, Neptune, and Pluto* by Caravaggio (1573–1610); and *Neptune Creates the Horse* by Jacob Jordaens (1593–1678).

BARBARA GARDNER

Bibliography
Homer, and Robert Fagles, trans. *The Odyssey*. New York: Penguin USA, 1999.
Pausanias, and Peter Levi, trans. *Guide to Greece*. New York: Viking Press, 1984.

SEE ALSO: Athena; Cronus; Gorgons; Neptune; Odysseus; Perseus; Sea; Theseus; Triton; Zeus.

INDEX

Page numbers in *italics* refer to picture captions. Page numbers in **bold** refer to main articles.